JANE BY THE SEA

Jane Austen's Love Story

CAROLYN V. MURRAY

Contact: carolynvmurray1@gmail.com
Visit Carolyn V. Murray's website at:
http://www.carolynvmurray.com

Cover design by Jane Dixon-Smith, JD Smith - Designs

ISBN: 978-0692429624
ISBN: 069242962X

Table of Contents

Prologue: 1787   1

Chapter 1: One Fateful Night   7

Chapter 2: Perfection   19

Chapter 3: A Bleak World   33

Chapter 4: The Splendor of Godmersham   47

Chapter 5: The Sea   65

Chapter 6: Dreadful Suitors   79

Chapter 7: A Surprising Twist of Fate   95

Chapter 8: The Return of Hope   109

Chapter 9: Too Good to Be True   123

Chapter 10: The Good Lie   139

Chapter 11: All Truths Revealed   151

Chapter 12: Waiting in Bath   169

Chapter 13: A Letter at Last   181

Chapter 14: Happy Endings   187

Post Script   201

Author's Note   203

PROLOGUE
1787

The mere prospect of opening my mouth to speak was enough to fill the room with cheers and clapping. Surely this was what it must feel like to be queen.

"Tell them *Jack and Alice* next," my little brother Charles commanded.

"Excellent choice," I agreed.

"Be quick. We only have ten minutes before your father gets back," another boy urged.

My father, the Reverend George Austen, was the headmaster of this small boarding school. In addition to Charles, there were seven other boys in attendance. The school was contained inside a narrow clapboard room that had always reminded me of a miniature church, but rather than pews, had a mismatched assortment of small tables and hard chairs formed in two rows.

At the end of a day, my father often gave them an assignment, and then disappeared for half an hour while the boys accomplished the task. But I would habitually trespass after some twenty minutes to see if they were all finished, and to ascertain whether they might benefit from a story of restless ghosts or violent retribution. Thankfully, they were

1

always eager for such diversions, and in truth, the benefit was mutual, for what are such tales without an audience? I gestured for silence and would not begin until it was had.

> *"Alice is the young headmistress of a shabby boarding school for girls. She has many rare and charming qualities, but ... sobriety is not one of them. She had already consumed half a bottle of rum, when she undertook a stroll in the nearby forest. It was a dark and treacherous place, but the rum had diminished her good judgment considerably, a frequent occurrence that often landed her in difficulties. Today, those difficulties came in the form of a steel bear-trap. SNAP!!! Her right foot was caught in its painful jaws."*

This turn of events delighted most of my young audience. However, one older boy yawned, almost certainly a purposeful attempt to annoy me. But I would tolerate neither boredom nor literary criticism. I should simply elevate the tale till it was beyond reproach. And years of entertaining a houseful of brothers and a classroom full of boys had instilled in me one cardinal rule: blood enhances every story.

Thus the snare proved to be so unforgiving that Alice's detached foot went flying through the air, bouncing unceremoniously off a nearby tree. My audience roared with laughter, and my detractor was put in his place. The tale continued with a peg-legged Alice sipping soup that had been laced with arsenic by her rival, Gertrude Wiley.

Though she staggered about in her seeming death throes, Alice was able to rally sufficiently to present herself at Gertrude's door, and the two of them came to such blows, as to compare with any bare knuckle fistfight in a London barroom brawl.

"But all ended well on a lovely summer day, when Alice had the satisfaction of watching the trap door open under Gertrude, whose neck was held fast by an obliging noose. It was such a violent motion, that one of her eyes popped out."

This ending received a big cheer, as expected. But the applause died out quickly, and I turned to the door to find the cause of it. There stood my mother and another lady of somewhat younger age, looking rather flustered. As for my mother ... she did not look entertained. Not in the slightest.

I had but a few hours to wait until my offenses were brought to trial. The place of reckoning was our large drafty barn. It was nearly the size of our house, and stuffed with tall stacks of hay I could not see over, sharp-edged harvesting tools, and a multitude of pungent animal pens. My father was engaged in milking the cows. He managed the task well, for he had long arms and strong hands. He also had a head full of white hair, as he was already at a seasoned age when I was born. But the long sharp features of his face seemed unchanging to me. And there was ever a good humoured smile hovering about him, awaiting the slightest provocation.

I busied myself with feeding our little weaned calves. My mother paced nearby. Often weary by this time of day, she was newly invigorated by my transgressions, and emphatically conveyed the events of the afternoon to my father. In younger days, I should have made myself scarce. But having reached the age of twelve, I did know that it was always best to be present to speak in one's own defense.

Frank, my elder brother by two years, made a show of clearing the barn floor of hay and droppings, but I was certain he was primarily there to be entertained by my scolding. He passed in front of me, and I put out a foot to trip him. He retaliated by "strangling" my neck, accompanied by the most grotesque facial contortions I could muster ... one of our favorite games.

How I would miss him. He was to leave in a fortnight to join the Royal Navy. Our older brothers had gone to Oxford University, but I gathered that we had run out of money for such things. Which left the military as the next best option. I was excited for him, but a bit downcast as well. One by one, each of four older brothers had left our home, and it was a sobering loss each time. We wrote to one another frequently, and as they had always enjoyed my silly tales of murder and mayhem, I was now obliged to commit my stories to pen to share with them. I intended to do the same for Frank, that he might have something to laugh at during a rare shipboard reprieve.

"Well, Mr. Austen. Have you nothing to say?" my mother demanded.

"Is *Jack and Alice* the one that ends with a hanging or a beheading?" Papa inquired.

"A hanging," I answered gleefully, which earned a glare from my mother.

"How are you so calm?" Mama fumed. "The widow Lancaster will now never consider schooling her boy here. And what is worse, we are likely to lose most of our present pupils."

"Really, my dear? How so?"

"One of those boys will surely report an account of this storytelling to his parents. They will withdraw him immediately and advise everyone they know to do the same."

"I think we need not trouble ourselves of that event," I ventured.

My mother was all skepticism, but my father was ever eager to hear the workings of my mind.

"And pray Jane, how goes your reasoning?"

"If a boy should inform his parents of the incident, we will denounce him as the worst of liars," I explained. "And no one will doubt the word of a clergyman. He will be disgraced in the eyes of his family, resulting in shame, loss of trust, estrangement, disinheritance, and ... suicide, surely."

My father's broad smile was as gratifying as the praise of an entire classroom. However, this performance also had its detractor.

"For shame, Mr. Austen," my mother scolded. "You know my bowels have been much irritated of late. She means to worsen them with this new vexation."

"Jane," my father urged, "If only for my sake, I beg you not to distress your mother's bowels."

I made a face at him. The Austen family had all been obliged to spend an ungodly amount of time contemplating the state of my mother's bowels. I thought my stories rather wholesome in comparison. But poor Mama could tell there was no sympathy to be had on this occasion, and she stormed away. No matter; I knew Papa would restore her spirits soon enough.

"What next, Jane? Decapitation? A haunted mansion?"

I had something else in mind: a sinister intrusion into polite society.

"A ball," I announced. "For though I have never been to one, I hear there is much opportunity for treachery and pandemonium."

It would be some years before I could test the truth of that statement.

CHAPTER ONE
ONE FATEFUL NIGHT

Flattering brown ringlets. A green satin gown, borrowed, but no less becoming. I gazed into the looking glass with keen approval. Well, what is the harm of that? After all, does modesty really serve a useful function when one is in a room all by oneself? Is it not an insincere spectacle whose effort should only be undertaken for the demands of society? Did history's great artists not have entitlement to a few smug solitary moments? Then why should the world begrudge me a small comforting self-assurance that my appearance tonight would please all but the most frightfully critical eye.

Tonight was the much anticipated ball at the Harwoods. And there was nothing I loved in the world so much as a ball. Not only for the dancing. Though that was no small thing. Where else can grown ladies and gentlemen leap and cavort like a magical return to childhood? But also for the noise, the crowds, the bustle ... ever in short supply in our little hamlet of Steventon. We had never had more than three and thirty families (in addition to four and twenty in neighboring Deane, and another fourteen at Ashe.) The town appeared to become quieter and drowsier with each passing year. And of late, it seemed as if my society had become unbearably small. My brothers had all gone ... to the clergy, to Oxford, to the Navy. The boarding school was disbanded. Papa had reached eight and sixty years, and with only two daughters left in the home, was able to make do with the stipend from the church, and the necessities provided by our own little farm.

But how I missed the clamoring din! The shoving, wrestling, boisterous chaos. And laughter. Always laughter in the air. Admittedly, most agreeable coming from an audience to my outlandish tales. In truth, I would never again know such appreciation. For while Papa was ever encouraging, my elder sister Cassie knew not what to make of my concoctions. And Mama would just as soon I set my pen down, and pick up a broom instead.

But the last and most indisputable blessing of the ball ... in the air of every such event hangs the possibility and the promise of matrimony. How could it be otherwise? The beauty, the music, the gaiety, the wine! The boon of one new face after another: visiting relations, soldiers on leave, sons, brothers, cousins, nephews. Unmarried. And as in need of a wife as I was of a husband.

Not that I considered it an urgent matter. I was but one and twenty. Quite young actually. Still, I should not like to be much older when I marry. Three and twenty at the very latest. If for no other reason, than Mama and I would come to blows if we were under the same roof for much longer than that. She continued to labor under the delusion that I could be molded into something more quiet and obedient and less like myself. And while I was not unwilling to do my share of the house's work, I was also entitled to spend time at my desk, scribbling my trifles. But she continually interrupted me. I realized they were of no importance, but in recent days, they were my only diversion.

How wonderful to be mistress of my own household. To choose the meals, command my own schedule, and order others about. Though my sister Cassie would ever be a welcome guest, what a blessed relief not to have her virtues laid alongside my vices for daily comparison. The freedom and independence of marriage! To say nothing of the bliss of sharing life with a man of such superior taste, intelligence, virtue, and wit that I had yet to lay eyes on such a creature. Oh, my father and brothers had spoiled me. For in them, I had seen that such qualities could exist, however scarce they generally were in Steventon. Where was such a man to be found? I took one last glance at my hopeful reflection. At a ball and nowhere else.

The chandeliers at the Harwoods' estate were enormous. They lit up a magnificent ballroom, large enough to hold a thousand people, though the party tonight numbered closer to two hundred. But the glittering glass, the flowers, the orchestra, the supper feast ... all planned with such care, received only my cursory regard. Exquisite, without question. But uppermost in my mind was a surveillance of the room's inhabitants. As well as to, ever so imperceptibly, escape the watchful gaze of my mother. I assembled with friends Martha Lloyd and Althea Bigg, and by unspoken consent, we inched ourselves away from my mother and her confidante, Mrs. Pratt. But while still within earshot, I detected a few last drops of conversation.

"I am so sorry your Cassandra did not come, Mrs. Austen," Mrs. Pratt sympathized.

"It would be to no purpose for her. After her fiancé died, she vowed never to marry," my mother explained. "Perhaps it is just as well, for she is a dear girl, and will be a great comfort to me in my old age. Jane, however, is unlikely to be a comfort, so it is best we marry her off."

Presumably it was a good thing that Mama and I were in agreement over something. Though still rather a hard thing to hear. In any case, I should no longer scruple to remain in the vicinity. Linking arms with Martha and Althea, we made our way to the far side of the room. Along the way, we ran a veritable gauntlet of anxious mothers, of single-minded determination, who had calculated the evening's matrimonial targets with the precision of a military campaign. From all sides, I heard the commands issued.

"You are stooping again, Penelope. Stand up! Stand up!"

"You are smiling too much, my dear. The gentlemen will find it very odd."

"Walk over to the punch bowl, Hermione. You must show your figure off to best advantage."

Posture. A pleasant smile. Oh, well. Let mothers and daughters alike enjoy these delusions. I was familiar with all of these girls and quite honestly, had little hope for their prospects. Penelope prided herself on producing the finest embroidery in the county. True, it was much admired, but would it ever make a gentleman's heart pound and incite a declaration of love? From my own direct encounters, I could state with certainty that she only had about five minutes of conversation to offer, and after it had been exhausted, getting further opinion or information from her was a painful extraction. My condolences to the man who falls in love with her posture.

On the other hand, I would have gladly silenced Hermione. Her weekly amusement on church Sundays was to inquire about my ongoing farm chores, in which she pretended to take a great interest. She herself had no farm chores, being the daughter of a very busy doctor, and a mother with a generous inheritance. But she did love to be kept abreast of how large our pigs had grown, and how weary my arms must have been from carrying the scraps to feed them, and was it time to pick the turnips yet, and how did this year's cabbage yield compare to the last? Was it really impossible to enjoy her life of relative ease without having to picture me in the muck? One consolation: she and I will never vie over the same gentleman, for any young man who shows her any partiality will have revealed such deficiencies in his own character and judgment that I could happily remove him from any consideration.

I was sure that I caught more than one envious glance from those captive girls as we sauntered through their midst and settled far, far away from my own matriarchal overseer. From that vantage point, we were able to commence the serious business of a head count. Single males to single females. The results, eight and twenty of the former, six and thirty of the latter, was received by Althea with defeat.

"Impossible! Jane, this is very bad news."

It would certainly be bad news. For some. For me, it signified nothing. Although eight ladies would be continually disappointed throughout the evening, I did not intend to be one of them. Martha smiled at my confidence. She took a keen and encouraging interest in my own pursuits. And wished for my success with her whole heart.

Some ten years older than myself, Martha had long ago adopted the severe hair and dark attire of a matronly aunt. She had quite resigned herself to her spinster's fate. I had never wanted her to feel badly on that score, but it did seem to me that a spinster lived a life somewhat suspended in childhood. And not the best, carefree aspects of early life. But, rather, an entire life under the same roof as your mother and father, subject to their preferences and commands, and surrounded by sameness for the entirety of one's whole life. Should the bed where you are read lullabies really be the same as your deathbed!? It was a troublesome prospect. And yet she was ever cheerful company, always a sympathetic ear, and when Cassie and I disagreed, Martha could be counted upon to take my side. As good as having another sister.

Across the room, I spotted an old crowd of familiar gentlemen. All married and above forty. But their connections were not to be underestimated. They might well provide introductions for their younger acquaintances. And if not, what were they doing here!!?

I excused myself and approached the men. I could not but be aware that a number of older ladies in the room would be fretting over my lack of decorum. Think what they will. *Someone* had to remind these gentlemen that they were at a dance, and the sight of a lady in a ball gown was the most effective aid.

As I drew near, I was not surprised to hear the gentlemen's minds were on war. This awful war with France had commanded our attention for the past four years. My brothers Frank and Charles were in the middle of it, having each enrolled in the Navy by the age of fourteen. The gentlemen conferred quietly.

"Have there not been heavy losses recently?"

"Yes, the last few months have been very hard."

"But, our advances have also been considerable. The Navy is particularly well-situated."

"And well-equipped, with the best of men," I interjected.

"Miss Austen, how to good to see you. Yes, were just speaking of His Majesty's Navy. I am sure they will play the greatest role in the final outcome."

"Well, I have done my part, for I have contributed two brothers to the cause. And there is so much talent between them, the Navy will have little choice but to prevail," I offered proudly.

One bemused gentleman responded, "Reason enough to dance," and led me away to the centre of the dancing. It was enjoyable enough, but I had made myself conspicuous, as I had anticipated. That sour Mrs. Mitford, shook her head and was most unwilling to take her eyes off of me. I could not imagine taking that degree of interest in *her* movements. Hah. If I were ever to write a story about her, I would have her shake that disapproving head of hers for so long that it should fall right off her shoulders!

I danced another four dances, two with single young men. But rather dull. And had my imagination run away, or was one of them actually frightened of me? "You are not for the faint of heart, my dear girl," Papa had said to me recently. Did he have no confidence in my marital prospects? It was, rather, Steventon's selection of men he should blame, which the war had thinned out considerably. But what is the proverb? All good things come to he who waits. Usually told to children to distract their minds from the things they want most. But tonight, this glorious, glorious night, those words were about to become the truest ever spoken.

When my mother signaled for me to join her, I could see that she was with our dear friend, Madame Anne Lefroy. I had thought to avoid my mother for a bit longer, but Madame Lefroy was a most welcome sight. Twenty six years my senior, I could not remember a time when I had not known her. We had had countless discussions on literature, art, philosophy, life. She spoke freely and encouraged me to do the same. She was my ideal of womanhood.

In fact, without sounding too horrid, if I should have had the misfortune of losing my mother at an early age, Madame Lefroy was the mother I would have longed for. An uncharitable thought perhaps. It was not that I did not have some appreciation for my mother's accomplishments. I was inordinately grateful for the fine collection of siblings she had provided me with. But her life seemed so consumed with practicalities: budgets, cleaning, and rationing of sugar. As well as tending to a multitude of imagined ailments. Still, I had to concede, she remained in as a good a humour as could be expected of a woman who had endured childbirth eight times. Madame Lefroy, however was a true kindred spirit. Like Martha Lloyd, she was regarded as dearly as family. As I approached, I could see that they were with a tall young man, whose pleasing features were only apparent as I came full upon them.

My mother pulled me closer. "Jane. Look who is here."

"Madame Lefroy. I am so glad you came."

Madame Lefroy gestured towards the young man. "My nephew gave me little choice in the matter. Jane. May I present Thomas Lefroy of Dublin. Tom ... Miss Jane

Austen."

A worthy introduction at last! We bowed.

"Tom has just begun his first year of legal studies in London." Madame Lefroy continued.

I was finally at liberty to address the young man, and I intended to take full advantage. "You time your visit well, Mr. Lefroy, for there are many balls planned these next few weeks."

Tom's Irish accent was like music. "I am glad to hear it. And may I look forward to the pleasure of sharing a waltz, Miss Austen?"

I thought I heard my mother gasp. No, the waltz and Steventon were little acquainted. Arms embracing, bodies touching! Cheeks, lips, only inches apart! I was sure I should be an old woman before Steventon sanctioned that sort of boldness. Poor Tom. I could not refrain from teasing him.

"A waltz! I'm afraid, Mr. Lefroy that you should never have left London if that sort of corruption and vice is necessary to your happiness."

My mother wanted to leave no doubt as to her opinion. "Indeed! No one but a woman's own husband is entitled to that intimacy."

"I am sure my mother would agree," Tom reassured. "However … the residents of London do seem differently inclined."

"Is it your intention, sir, to drag our town into urban depravity?" I inquired.

Tom's smile was a dizzying ray of sunshine. "Miss Austen, are you engaged for the next two dances?"

And so it began. As I floated to the dance floor, I marveled at how quickly I felt at ease in his company. We did not hesitate to speak freely.

"Is Hampshire free of all sinful enjoyments?" he asked.

"We do boast a few modest offenses."

"And which is your particular favorite? Gambling? Intoxication?"

"Far worse, I'm afraid. But it is without shame that I lay my vice bare. I am an unrepentant reader of novels."

He gasped, feigning horror. "No!"

"Yes."

"I can scarcely believe it."

"An activity so fraught with unsavory influence, that even our town librarian continually apologizes for the inclusion of novels in her establishment."

With that came a break in the music, and we retired to a quiet corner.

"And what have your parents to say? What says your father, a *clergyman*, of the moral deficiency implicit in such a habit?"

"Ah, there I can acquit myself. For what blame should I own, when I was raised so ill?"

"You don't mean to say …?"

"Yes, both of them. All of them. A whole family of novel readers."

"Good Lord. And I must presume, that these practices have driven at least one of your relations into a sanitarium."

"A reasonable assumption, sir, but no, such is not the case."

"Then your poor family must have been torn asunder by adultery; for that is the logical influence of these heinous tales of fancy and temptation."

"Adultery?"

Our volume had risen. Several heads swiveled in our direction.

"No, not to my knowledge. But perhaps, I ought to make inquiries at the dinner table tomorrow night. For such activities could easily have escaped my notice ... whilst my head was buried in a book."

We beamed; the enchantment was mutual.

There is a wall of polite discourse that you encounter any time you step away from your family. I was quite familiar with these laws of conduct, and didn't find them overly oppressive. They could, in fact, be manipulated to some advantage. Certainly, with the young gentlemen I have met (and I was ever asking the same question ... is he the one?) I could exert myself to make favorable impressions and censor the most tantalizing and untoward of thoughts. However, to keep up that pretense indefinitely? A daunting prospect. But here before me was a young man who delighted in my every impulse. With him the restraints of polite society were swept away. And as if that were not enough, how handsome he was!!

When I glanced over at Madame Lefroy, eager to share my happiness, I was somewhat taken aback by the agitation on her face. Oh, dear. As fond as she was of me, she was as wed to decorum as any other in her social class, and a young lady and gentleman of such recent acquaintance were not permitted to show such fierce partiality for one another.

Dance followed dance. One tête-à-tête begat another. Tom spoke fondly of Dublin, the beauty of the surrounding countryside, and the warm-hearted people he grew up amongst. I admit I had never given two moments thought to Dublin, but if he was from Dublin, then Dublin it would be. For in the space of less than half an evening, I could feel that this man was my destiny. I had never anticipated such a thunderbolt of certainty. But in my mind's eye, I could see our small estate, our lovely grounds. And the companionship of his sisters, who numbered as many as my brothers.

Not that I would be able to do without my Cassie. She must visit often and for long periods of time. In fact, whenever I should have a child, she could come for three or four months at a time to assist. What an exhilarating thought! Children. With this man! I was overtaken with visions of domestic bliss.

Two hours passed in this manner, till Madame Lefroy prompted Tom's reluctant departure. No matter. The joyous expectation of the evening did not die in his absence. I felt it swell and gave no thought to checking it. Had it all really happened? It was as if I had dreamed some impossibly happy vision, and drawn it with my own hand.

CHAPTER TWO
PERFECTION

I rose late the next day. Cassie had already gone out, and Papa was about his chores. I paced the house with an excess of energy, until Mama's irritation drove me back into my bedroom. A room cozy enough, with one bed large enough for two sisters, and penciled family portraits lining the walls. There, to wait for Cassie. How would she receive my wondrous news? Dear Cassie. Poor Cassie. How would the tale of someone else's love fall on her shattered heart?

She still wore clothes of mourning, it being less than a year since her fiancé, Thomas Fowle, had died of cholera overseas. They had been betrothed for four years and were but four months away from a wedding day. He had accepted a position as Naval chaplain, in order to amass a respectable sum on which to begin their household. Thomas, Thomas, Thomas. What happiness he brought her. And how we had all loved him for it.

Now, at four and twenty, Cassie resembled nothing so much as a widow. She pushed aside all suggestions of future love. She was resigned to solitude and grief. Natural, of course, with the loss so fresh and so deep. But surely, she would learn to be more hopeful and find love again. She had to. For there was no more deserving creature on this whole earth.

When she returned, I was anxious to relay the events of the previous evening. In exchange for abuse of her ear, she required that I sit quietly for a sketch, one of her few remaining pleasures.

"It was the most wonderful, momentous night of my existence," I enthused.

"Jane, I was in the village this morning. Your behavior at the ball has exposed you to many impertinent remarks," Cassie cautioned.

"From whom, pray tell? Mrs. Mitford? Who was most fortunate to have a dowry of 20,000 for no one could have been persuaded to marry her for fourpence less."

"*And* others. Take care, Jane. As it is possible that you may cause offense to the same gentlemen you most wish to impress."

"If there had been any real impropriety in what I did, I should have been sensible of it."

"I do not know whether you and I could reach agreement on that point."

At this moment, I had to leap up from my seat and grab Cassie by the shoulders.

"Envision the most shocking and indecent scene of dancing, followed by, I blush to recall, sitting down and *conversing!* Oh, yes. And then, what do you think? Why we got up and danced again, and *then* … here you may well take me to task … why we sat down and conversed *yet again!*"

Cassie could only shake her head at my effusions.

"Indeed, there has been talk in the Church of starting a charitable concern for girls who dance too much."

At this, Cassie headed for the stairs, hoping to put an end to my ranting. Hah! I was close on her heels.

"They will be housed in cell rooms so small that even a clandestine jig will be all but impossible. And further, there should also be a separate isolation ward for those who, in addition, are prone to excessive conversation."

"I should pay good tax money to support such an institution," Cassie responded.

In the sitting room, Papa had returned from his chores, and was mulling over his sermon for the coming Sunday. He looked up at our noisy entrance.

"Well, my dear. I am glad to hear you enjoyed yourself last evening. Though, I am sure you have had your fill of dances for the season, and will not need to attend another until spring."

How could he suggest such a thing? Even in jest, it was a distressing thought. "Quite so Papa, and it is equally likely that I shall not need my next bite of food either, until spring," I replied.

Without hesitation, he turned to my sister. "Cassandra. Inform the cook."

Cassie was always glad when my wild impulses met their match. "I should like to see you a little faint from hunger in order to still you for my portrait."

I settled down at my little writing table. "Then you had best take advantage right now, for I am sitting down to write."

Cassie pulled out her sketch book. "A good long letter, I hope."

"No, a new story."

My father was glad to hear it. "Indeed! And what is the tale?"

"It is about two sisters. Elinor and Marianne … who shall find their happy matches after much misunderstanding."

"How much misunderstanding?" Cassie inquired.

"No more than sixty pages worth, for I shall then be out of paper."

"And what of the father? Probably a wise, useful old fellow, eh?" my father suggested expectantly.

"Dead. By page two."

My father looked a bit affronted.

"A little poverty is required to set events into motion," I explained.

"Hmmph!" He made an exaggerated show of returning to his sermon.

It was Cassie's turn to wonder about her own contribution. "And what of the sisters? I suppose the elder one is very dull."

"Not at all. But she is very sensible and prudent. Likewise her courtship will be *very* sensible and *very* prudent."

"Elinor Dashwood and Edward Ferrars had known one another but three weeks before their mutual regard became an undeniable fact. But while their passion spilled to the brim, they had the good sense to confine their conversation to the weather, religion, and agriculture. Any outward display of affection would have been unseemly. Thus, after Elinor poured the

afternoon tea, and turned her head to have a word with the maid, Edward, who could not even allow himself the liberty of holding Elinor's hand, took the utmost pleasure in communing with items that had been blessed by her touch. He fondly caressed the teapot with his cheek, until a searing sensation and subsequent scream of pain brought him back to his senses.

As for Marianne Dashwood and her suitor John Willoughby, they were heedless of society's good opinion, and let their love run loose as a wild stallion. On the ballroom floor, their bodies were inseparable; the waltz was designed for their unshakeable devotion. In fact, one hapless gentleman, who interrupted them with the unfortunate intent of claiming a dance, was rewarded for his impertinence by a heated encounter with Willoughby's fist, followed by a singularly unobstructed view of the ballroom ceiling."

"Preposterous," Cassie interrupted.

"I am only working out the details," I defended.

My father chimed in, "A fine start, my dear."

At that moment, my mother bustled into the room. "Jane! Young Mr. Lefroy is coming down the road!"

I leapt to my feet, unable to curtail my excitement. Cassie sighed and tucked her sketchbook away. Though her eyes cautioned me to exercise restraint, the entire family could not but be aware, that a young man coming to call could only be a prelude to matrimony.

We were allowed to convene with some measure of privacy in our small library. Tom's young cousin Philip had been sent along to act as chaperone. He sat in a corner of the room, watching us intently. As for the man himself, he was a fine figure in his white waistcoat (impractical, but he was obviously unused to life in the country.) We continued as we had left off, his charm and warm ease as evident as the night we had met. He was enjoying his first year of law school in London, which was being financed by his great uncle, Mr. Benjamin Langlois, a notable member of Parliament. He did miss his home in Dublin though, where he had five unmarried sisters yet living at home. No doubt, his upbringing in a houseful of women, and mine in a houseful of men accounted for a good deal of our ease with one another. Further, we shared the delight of two minds excited by education … his directly, and mine by proximity to Oxford trained father and brothers. A more perfect match could not have been imagined.

I walked him around a cluster of family portraits on the wall. We stopped in front of the most imposing.

"And who has earned such a place of distinction on your walls?"

It was my brother, Edward Knight. Formerly Edward Austen. Until, when at the age of ten, he was selected heir by distant relatives with no child of their own. Adopted right out of our family and into theirs. We missed him, of course. As we missed each brother who made his way out into the world. But no one could question the wisdom of this new family allegiance. I was fond of the Austen name, but it was an easy sacrifice in return for a fortune. Tom was in utter agreement.

"Indeed, I would give up Lefroy for one thousand a

year. No! Half that!"

But that was a prick to his young cousin's familial pride. He scowled at us, unamused. Oh, why should our discourse be dictated by the sensibility of a nine year old child?

"Philip, if you run to the kitchen, I think the cook may be able to find some nice sweetmeats for you," I suggested brightly.

"But I am supposed to watch cousin Tom," the pixie replied.

Tom drew his little cousin closer to the door.

"And an excellent chaperone you have been. But if you do not nourish yourself, you will grow weak and lose your concentration. Your capacity to fulfill your duties will be sadly compromised. Off you go."

And with that, Philip was pushed out of the room. What a quick mind he had, this future husband of mine.

"Is that the sort of irrefutable logic you will draw on in your duties as a barrister?"

"I shall win case after case with these same powers of persuasion. Do you doubt it?"

"What I cannot believe is that you are going to spend your time making accusations, provoking defensive counter-attacks, and being argumentative. And to be paid for it!"

"Should you like to spend your time in this manner?"

"I already do. But no one thinks to pay me for it!"

Tom strolled along a wall of books, a rather impressive collection, I was proud to note.

"And how many of these books have you read?"

"Easier to count the ones I have not."

Tom pulled one volume out. "Here is one you will not have read, and I must say, I did not expect to find it in a clergyman's collection."

"As a matter of fact, I read that first at age fourteen, and many times since," I boasted.

"Your father allowed you to read *Tom Jones*? And at fourteen?!!"

"My father is a busy man, with far more important things on his mind than my literary habits."

"And ... what did your fourteen year old mind think when Tom Jones happened to spend the night with his very own 'mother?'"

"I thought it very ... odd."

We could not contain our delight at this forbidden exchange. How mundane, how dreary other mortals were alongside this man. What a glorious gift had entered my life. What freedom and abandon we could enjoy together. Free to create a world outside of society. And above it. Thank goodness I had never been tempted to attach myself to some lesser man. For was anything on earth so worth the wait?

When I was not with him, I could but talk of him. The following morning while shopping in town, I was compelled to share my felicity with Martha and Cassie.

"I did not think to ever find a gentleman who could satisfy my notion of perfection."

"Is there nothing about him that falls short of excellence?" Martha inquired.

I considered. "His coat should be a darker shade. But there his flaws begin and end."

"Martha, can you not persuade her to be more reasonable?" Cassie pleaded.

"I think Jane will make an excellent barrister's wife. But, shall you live in Ireland or London?"

"Thank you Martha ... for *your* good wishes."

Cassie brought our walk to a halt. "Just a moment, Jane. I must say hello to Mrs. Ellington."

We looked across the street to see Mrs. Ellington, six months heavy with child, with six children, ages two to twelve, trailing her. A not unfamiliar sight, that always led me to shudder.

"Good God. How can that woman honestly be breeding again?"

"I am sure she considers it a great blessing," Cassie scolded.

Children may very well be a blessing. I was sure I would be very fond of my first and second child. Perhaps I shall even be in good humor after the third. But I had seen too much evidence around me of families swollen to frightening size, and women whose bodies and spirits were forever wrecked.

"It is her tenth child! There can be no occasion to abuse a poor woman's reproductive organs in this manner."

"But how is it to be helped?" Martha shrugged.

"A simple regimen of separate bedrooms would do the trick."

"And just when should a family apply this strategy? After the fourth child? After the sixth?" my sister inquired sternly.

"Certainly after the sixth! That is strain enough for any woman."

"Except, that you are a seventh child, and dear Charles is number eight. Do you not think that it was advisable for Mama and Papa to increase our family to its full size?"

While glad my parents had not followed *my* sound inclinations, I was yet unready to concede the argument.

"In hindsight, those *were* wise additions. But there is no ninth, tenth, or twelfth, and I daresay, we have not suffered from their absence."

We found ourselves in front of a dress store, with an enticing display in the window. Martha and I sighed longingly. But she would not go in. Her circumstances were even more constrained than our own, and she could not bear the thought of being tormented by expensive clothes that were beyond her reach. We parted ways, with plans to rejoin soon after.

Inside the shop, the unending selection of brilliant fabrics had the effect on me of half a dozen glasses of wine. We were two weeks away from the last ball of the season, and it was to be at Ashe, the Lefroy family home! If I could dazzle Tom on that occasion, who knows, but that I would not incite a proposal on that very same night. I did not appreciate being pulled out of these musings by Cassie, who continued to caution me on my deportment. My deportment! As seen from the vantage point of the gossiping Mrs. Mitford.

"If you want to satisfy yourself on my behaviour, you will have to attend the next dance with me. Though Althea Bigg may never forgive me for bringing you, for you are quite pretty enough to divert the attention of all the most eligible bachelors."

"You know I no longer take interest in dances."

Cassie had not only lost her fiancé, but youth and hope as a well. She embraced grief as a lifelong companion. I could not allow it.

"Cassie. Mr. Fowle was a very fine man. But even

widows have been known to find love again. And you are not even a widow."

Cassie's hand flew to her throat, where her hand found her daily comfort: a locket, containing a handsome miniature of the man who would have been her husband.

"For four years, I enjoyed the pleasure of his company, and the comfort of his devotion. I am nothing but grateful for it. And I will not engage in a vain search to find its equal. I have already had the best that love has to offer ... and it is enough."

But she would not burden others. She steered me toward the bins of cloth. "So, my dear Jane, all matrimonial efforts are now to be directed on your behalf. Here ..."

Her selection was a pretty blue cotton print. Nice enough for an afternoon party. But hardly something that would inspire a man to drop to his knees and profess undying love. But, oh! There was a heavenly pink silk cloth that caused everything around it to fade to a dull grey hue. My search was over.

"Jane. You haven't the money," Cassie protested.

"Just enough."

"And what will you live on for four months till your next allowance?"

On love, of course.

Despite her reservations, Cassie could be depended upon to help make the dress. Mama, as well. The prospect of my removal from the Austen family was a cherished dream of hers. In fact, that night of the ball, as I arrived at Ashe in my exquisitely cut gown, she and I were truly and finally of one mind.

As I stepped inside the walls of Ashe, I breathed in the sanctified air of the Lefroy family ... soon to be my kin! Not so grand a home as the Harwoods, but ever so much dearer to me.

Tom was already on the ballroom floor. I knew his partner well. Poor girl. I could tell from the dazzled expression on her face that she was suffering from an excess of unrequited enthusiasm. Poor Tom. As a member of the family, his social obligations tonight would be considerable. No matter. I knew the lion's share of the evening would be saved for me.

Madame Lefroy came over to greet us.

"Mrs. Austen. And Jane. How nice to see you. You see, I thought the ball would be a splendid way for Tom to end his visit, for he will be off to London tomorrow."

Surely, I did not hear her correctly. "Tomorrow! That cannot be. For, is he not to stay another fortnight?"

"His plans have altered, and his family requests his immediate return to town."

"This is most unfortunate news," Mama fussed. "He will return in the spring, surely."

"I do not think so," Madame Lefroy replied apologetically.

"The summer, then?"

"I am sure he will be wanted at home."

"But if he has a reason to return to Hampshire, I am sure his family will not object."

"Tom ... must be exceedingly mindful of his obligations to his family. He is indebted to his uncle, Mr. Benjamin Langlois, and Tom must repay him one day. Tom also has five unmarried sisters, with uncertain futures. He must provide well for them."

I finally regained my voice. "That he shall certainly do."

Madame Lefroy turned to me gently, with much kindness in her expression. Although in later days, I was to remember it as pity. "He must improve his security in all respects. He owes it to his family."

Her tone suggested a deficit, but with these new qualities laid before me, he could only rise in my esteem.

With the last dance just ended, Tom was finally free to join us. "Mrs. Austen. Miss Austen. So pleased you could come."

I had never seen him so somber. I could only imagine that our premature separation was weighing as heavily on his mind as on my own. My mother brought the matter to the forefront.

"Tom, we are so sad to hear you will be leaving so soon. I'm sure you and Jane must try to enjoy your last night of dancing together."

Tom turned red. "I am, unfortunately, engaged for another six dances. But it will be my pleasure to share a dance with Miss Austen before the end of the evening. If you will excuse me." And with a stiff bow, he was gone.

What a chill descended on me. From the first moments of our acquaintance, there had been nothing between us but warm and mutual regard, that grew measurably with every encounter. Why then, had he just greeted me as a person of the lightest familiarity? The only sensation more intoxicating than my own feelings had been the certainty that he shared them. How could such conviction vanish in an instant?

"Do sit down Jane," Mrs. Lefroy urged. "You look a bit tired." I was not tired. I was dizzy. And trembling. And my heart pounded with such apprehension, one might think I was being led to the Tower.

Our dance, when it did occur later in the evening, was characterized on his part by cordiality and evasion. My questions went all unanswered. My endearments were met with sad deflections. Why such reserve? Even as our hearts became attached, we had known that we must endure many separations while he completed his education. Now, his departure was to be unexpectedly abrupt; all the more reason to shower one another with comforting reassurances. Why then, could he not meet my eye?

Along the wall, my mother and Madame Lefroy were engaged in conversation, the content of which was not relayed to me until weeks later. One of Tom's inescapable family obligations was the expectation that he would marry well. Which is to say, to a woman of good fortune. Word of our increasing affection had reached his Great Uncle Langlois. It was he who hastened Tom's departure, and advised Madame Lefroy to remind Tom, in the strongest of terms, of the imperative of finding a suitable wife.

To the Honorable Mr. Langlois, I was but a penniless clergyman's daughter, a low and unworthy candidate for marriage. I had never learned to regard myself in this manner. How had my dearest Tom been brought so quickly to see me thus? Can there be anything true about love if I could be cherished and then forsaken in the space of mere days?

Never before had a single moment so clearly separated one portion of life from another. My girlhood ended that night, as I felt love seep away, like blood from an unstoppable wound.

CHAPTER THREE
A BLEAK WORLD

I should be ashamed to admit how long I carried that sorrow. I, who regularly counseled my sister against keeping alive a truly unbearable loss. But admit it I must, for anything less would be distasteful falsehood. I spent countless hours at the pianoforte, perfecting every doleful Irish ballad I could lay my hands upon. I walked long and daily, in all manner of weather, to be alone with my demon thoughts of the happy life in Ireland that should have been my fate. And I avoided the village, well aware that I had become the object of much gossip and derision. Weekly attendance at church was more than enough society, and owing to Papa's obligations, unavoidable.

I could only curse my vivid imagination, for it had created the most exquisite and torturously indelible vision of happiness and destiny. The face, the unknown face that I had carried around these last few years had finally been etched in. Tom's face had now been implanted in my mind, and was as deeply embedded as my vital organs.

Had I the opportunity to meet Mr. Langlois directly, and

had he the chance to see me as a person rather than as a thought … could I have charmed him into a reversal of sentiment? Even so, could I ever truly forgive Tom for giving me up?

Did he ever think of me? Did he ever speak of me? Perhaps all could be forgiven if I knew that he suffered my loss horribly. Or was he blithely perfecting his waltz with the pretty young ladies of London? It was a prospect that left me doubled over like a blow to the midsection.

If the joy and expectation lasted but three weeks, why should the pain linger at such disproportionate length? I could more easily have recovered from a putrid illness. Or broken bones.

Or both.

And what of my writing? My giddy tales of love's inevitable triumph? They lay at my desk abandoned. As abandoned as I. But my father had a scheme to pull me back into good spirits.

"Jane, dear, it has been some time, has it not, since you have worked on your stories? And they gave you such pleasure."

"I am out of paper, and out of money, Papa. And I have not the heart for fanciful tales."

His reply was to hold out a stack of some fifty sheets of paper.

"Here is something I hoped you could use. Yes? And a stint of writing can only do you good. I am sure of it. Go and write a jolly scene, eh?"

Perhaps it *was* wrong to leave a story untold. Elinor and Marianne's live were suspended in the air. And they were to be the first beneficiaries of my newfound insight into the human condition.

Marianne Dashwood lay in bed, eyes closed. Elinor knelt over her, distraught. The doctor stood close by.

Elinor pleaded, "Please, Marianne. You must rally. You must get well. I know you are strong. I know you will conquer this."

The doctor leaned over Marianne, taking her pulse, and turning gravely to Elinor.

"I am very sorry to tell you this, Miss Dashwood. Your sister is dead."

"That is impossible! It cannot be true. It cannot be!"

"Oh, it is quite possible. For was she not recently bitterly disappointed in love?"

"No! Yes! But it is not possible to die of a broken heart."

"Ah, but there is the proof."

With a sob, Elinor flung herself over Marianne's body. The doctor shook his head sadly.

It took but a few more words to end the Dashwoods' tale. A sparsely attended funeral. And Miss Elinor Dashwood was left to face solitude and spinsterhood with commendable resignation. Such is life. I was done with fairy tales. At least I could claim *that*.

◇◇◇

Much time passed, with little incident. My family's circumstances sank precariously low at times, but were sustained through the generosity of half a dozen brothers and kin, scattered wide, but never forgetting us.

My house and garden duties were increased. My mother had arrived at the sad conclusion that I was to be a permanent fixture and that my usefulness must be maximized. I had little protest. With my mind directed elsewhere, my scars were free to heal without my constant poking and prodding.

One day, home from church, we exited the carriage and my father called the driver aside. His voice was subdued, and we all lingered outside the house, until their business was concluded, and my father rejoined us.

"He is a good fellow. I am sure he will find employment."

My heart sank. "Find employment?"

"The carriage has become too great an expense. I am afraid it must be given up," my father explained.

Give up the carriage! The last bit of pleasantry and convenience in our increasingly circumscribed situation.

"It was a pleasant thing," Cassie offered, "But we got on quite well for many years without it."

I glared at her. This was no time for her cheerfulness. The future was looking truly dreary. No husbands. No dowries. No inheritance. And something more troubling beneath it all. The fact of the matter was that my father was deeply in debt and had been for decades, even before my birth. How oblivious I had been. But though the extent of our difficulties had been hidden from me, I had no doubt that others must know. It was such a small community. What was being said about the Austens and their shameful debt?

A BLEAK WORLD

◇◇◇

The following week, life continued its downward spiral. After church, I waited impatiently outside with Cassie and Martha as Papa was occupied with talking to parishioners. It was full a year since I had last seen Tom Lefroy, and I had been made aware that he had returned to visit his aunt for the holidays. The busy tongues of Steventon were delighted to note that he had not troubled himself to call on Miss Jane Austen. Who could ever forget what a spectacle she made of herself last year? Did I still feel the loss? Very much. So much so that gossip and humiliation inflicted a vastly lesser sting, and I had come to disregard them.

Madame Lefroy never mentioned Tom, but treated me with great gentleness. Although she was a painful reminder of the worst episode of my life, I could not blame her for a decision that was never in her hands. Had it been, I truly believe I would have been welcomed to the Lefroy family with open arms.

As we waited for Papa, we were approached by Mr. Holder, a gentleman of fifty, on very good acquaintance with my father. He carried a bundle of newspapers, which he quietly offered us, and which I accepted reluctantly. It was a cutting reminder that the Austens could not afford their own subscription.

But I could not pass up the opportunity to read about the latest military developments. Life revolved around news of the war, which was sobering, whether good or bad. For the good news would reach our ears some two or three months after the incident. And our dark anxieties were forever wondering what setbacks and losses had been experienced in

37

the interim. Particularly troubling was my growing awareness that the Royal Navy in which I took such pride had an aging and rotting fleet of ships, and staffed close to half its crews with criminals straight from the prison system!

"That was most kind of him," Martha remarked.

"True," I acknowledged. "Still, I had rather administer charity than be the object of it."

"That is not a good way to think about it," Cassie scolded. "There can be no occasion to waste good money on a subscription when such resources can be so easily and generously shared ..."

Cassie's voice faded away, although I was fairly certain that she continued to speak. The words in the newspaper commanded my full attention, and in a daze, I wound up at my father's elbow.

"What is it, Jane? Can it not wait?"

I pulled him unceremoniously away from his companions, and thrust the story under his eyes. As he read, my mind seized on chaotic images of sailors turning on their own comrades. Dozens run through with swords. Scores thrown overboard. A cataclysmic mutiny that had touched every corner of the Royal Navy. My father finally looked up, his face torn between his fears and his desire to comfort.

"It was only a few days ago that we received Charles' letter. He is quite well. I am sure," he said firmly.

"But ... Frank's last letter?" I stammered.

"Some two months ago," he admitted. "I am sure his next letter will be most exciting. He will be able to give us a full account of these events. If he is aware of them at all. For it is likely his ship was wholly unaffected."

But my expression must have conveyed my panic.

"Patience and prayer are the best tools at our disposal.

They are the gifts that allow us to endure our fears and uncertainties," he continued.

I refused the comfort. "You are at work on your next sermon," I countered bitterly.

"I am never out of faith. And neither should you be," he chided gently.

Our words and minds were so disparate. But our hearts had fallen to an identical abyss. The prospect of losing Frank could never be spoken aloud. Though I loved all my brothers, I cannot truthfully maintain that all were loved equally. Did I think that Tom Lefroy had broken my heart? I knew better now. My heart had yet to be irrevocably destroyed. A letter of condolence from the Navy would have sent the entire Austen family to our graves. Papa and I wrapped our arms around each other, and stood motionless in the bustling churchyard.

I learned to take comfort from wherever I could find it ... largely in the beauty of the Hampshire countryside. What peace was to be found in those crooked rolling hills that surrounded our home. Even in the last of winter, with barren trees, a fresh layer of snow added such sweet beauty, that I was cheered in spite of myself. It was in these fine spirits that I arrived home one afternoon, to find my brother James and his wife Mary, at tea with our parents.

Of all my brothers, James has always had the least inclination to indulge me. His choice of wife separated us still further. Mary was Martha Lloyd's sister, but nothing like her, and we suffered one another from a careful distance. But though she and I were never at ease, she suited my brother well. And not surprisingly, she was a great favorite with my mother.

Their visit was unexpected; I greeted them with surprise. There was a brief, suspenseful pause as all eyes in the room focused on me and my anticipated reaction.

"Jane, there is excellent news," my mother proclaimed. "Your father is to retire and James is to take over his living. And we are to move to Bath in three weeks time. Are you not delighted?"

Years later, it became Austen family lore that my response to this news was to faint on the spot. I have always denied it. I cannot remember precisely what happened next, but I cannot bear to own to such weakness. There *was* a headache that lasted for some time after, but I was sure it resulted from the shock, rather than an encounter with the floor.

The next three weeks, I wandered about in a Catholic purgatory. My home was as dear to me as a living parent. The kitchen, the grounds, my room … cast out of Paradise! And what was my crime? My behavior of late had, for lack of opportunity, been relatively blameless. There were certainly no young men in Steventon who tempted any breach of propriety. Perhaps my mind and tongue continued their recklessness in the safe company of Martha and Cassie, but in public, I had made an admirable attempt to counterfeit a tolerable decorum. I had done nothing to deserve this coming exile. My family was wholly oblivious to our impending loss.

Moreover, I felt as if I was not only losing my home, but was in danger of losing a part of myself. Bath was so excessively staid and genteel. Should I even remain the same person? What if the society of Bath exerted an overpowering conformity? And what of my wild, silly stories? They would be no more at home in Bath than I. Perhaps they were indigenous to Steventon and would reject Bath as an unnatural habitat. What should I do then?

My father approached his seventieth year, and I could not deny that he deserved more restful days. The demands of the school had been wearing on him heavily when he decided to close it just a few years back. Oh, how sad I was to see the boys leave. But Papa's burdens were considerably lightened, and we all adjusted, unhappily, to the reduced income. I came to be thankful that my own formal education had been so lacking, else there was a real danger that Mama would have condemned me to seek work as a governess. Thankfully, my French, arithmetic, Latin, and piano were sufficiently inadequate.

I could not fault Papa. To do any one thing for forty years was a mighty accomplishment. I should not like to see him overtax himself, now that the problems of age presented themselves with greater and greater frequency. Tending to the needs of his parishioners and our little farm were certainly fatiguing. But why could we not find some way to remain in Steventon? Could we not build another house for James and his family? Or add some additional rooms? As little as I liked the prospect of sharing a roof with Mary, it was certainly preferable to banishment.

But something else was afoot. It was never discussed. No one would admit to it. And the very thought of it made my cheeks burn for the role I had played in sealing my own doom. For it was my sister's and my own failure to attain matrimonial security that led my parents so eagerly down the road to Bath. All prospects in Steventon had been exhausted. The large society of Bath and its considerable supply of unmarried young men presented the last best hope for their spinster daughters. The undercurrent of resignation and pity was too much for me.

My sister-in-law Mary went to extraordinary lengths to annoy me. Under the guise of assistance, she packed up our belongings to hurry us out of the house. In the kitchen, she cast a calculating eye on the utility of our collections.

"Does your mother intend to take the china with her?" Mary inquired disingenuously.

"Oh heavens, yes," Cassie replied. "It has been in her family for generations."

"Of course. It is only that, it may be broken on the journey. It would be such a terrible waste. And so distressing."

"You think of our every comfort," I responded, through gritted teeth. I had no desire to disguise my meaning.

I took even fewer pains later with Martha, in the certainty that her love for me superseded any sisterly loyalties. She kept Cassie and me company as we fed the pigs.

"I hope that your sister will find Steventon a comfortable home," offered Cassie, with her usual irritating courtesy.

"Can she ever love this place the way we have?" I ranted. "Our crooked hills … our ancient trees … the crackle of dry leaves underfoot when strolling down the lane in autumn."

"It is not everyone who has your passion for dead leaves," Cassie responded, trying to conceal her smile. I glared at her.

"Our beautiful home. In *her* hands!"

Cassie chided, "Jane! Have you no care for Martha?"

Martha gave me a reassuring wink. "I confess, I am fonder of Jane than of my sister. Abuse her to your heart's content."

I needed no further encouragement. "They rush us out like common tenants," I groused.

Cassie countered, "But while our new home undergoes improvements, it is an excellent opportunity to visit Edward, now that he has taken possession of Godmersham. Jane, I wish you would reconsider."

It was true. Under all normal circumstances, I would have leapt at the chance to visit Edward and bask in the luxury of his new estate. But my parents and Cassie had worn me down with their cheerfulness and pretense. And I could tolerate no more.

"No, I am most happy to avail myself of Martha's hospitality for the next two months. It is better I be removed from my dear family for the present time, for they destroy my last shred of happiness and expect me to smile."

Cassie shook her head helplessly at Martha as she backed away to leave. "Do not forget, Jane. Regardless of your feelings, we must still think of a good welcome present for Mary."

Hmmm. What about a stick to beat her with? Martha smiled broadly, as if my thought had been spoken out loud.

◇◇◇

In the interim period, before my family's departure, I did my best to avoid their exhortations to join them. My most frequent means of evasion was to keep company with Agnes, our cook, in the kitchen. Which served a double purpose. Agnes was not to accompany us to Bath, for her expense had become too great a strain. I got a bit teary-eyed at the thought of never seeing her again. However, she was so brusque and familiar with me, that I would never admit such a thing. My rationale for avoiding Godmersham was incomprehensible to her.

"Passin' up a chance to stay at your brother's grand house! For heaven's sake! They say it has eight and twenty rooms!" Agnes cast a probing eye in my direction. "I'll be deviled if I can understand such a silly decision. Not unless you had a particular reason to stay here."

"And what would that be?" I scoffed. "Perhaps you think I cannot absent myself from all this fine cuisine."

"Oh, to be sure … or a young man, perhaps," she mused.

I snorted at the notion. "I am quite familiar with all the young men in this neighborhood. They are an ambitious group, I will give them that. And most hope to rise in life by marrying a woman of some fortune."

"Ah, it is a shame you are not acquainted with *very* wealthy men," Agnes responded.

I was confused. "Very wealthy men?"

She subsequently began to enlighten me with the tale of a widower she had worked for in Leeds. He owned so much land that it required three days to walk it from end to end. And who had this wealthy and influential man decided to marry? Why, his governess! But why should that be such a surprise, Agnes reasoned, when he was devoted to her, and had plenty of money for them both.

It was a jolting revelation for me. While I owned up to longing for a number of creature comforts, and freedom from nagging money concerns, I had never targeted my marital search in the direction of wealth. In fact, I had scorned such shallow and debased motives for a union. But here was a new wrinkle. One with irrefutable merit.

"A *very* wealthy man does not have to marry to *improve* his situation," I enthused. "He is free to marry for love."

Agnes nodded grudgingly, allowing me to take the credit for a discovery that was, in fact, her own.

I ignored my parents' looks of amazement as I dragged my small trunk out and heaved it in the rear of the carriage. I was disinclined to explain myself. My swift and imminent success in Godmersham would be all the explanation necessary. And would render Bath a moot point.

CHAPTER FOUR
THE SPLENDOR OF GODMERSHAM

I had once visited the Godmersham estate, very shortly after Edward was adopted by the Knights. As a rule, time and maturity generally render the awe-inspiring objects of childhood mundane and unimpressive. Godmersham was the great exception. My adult eyes and mind were even better able to comprehend the dazzling display and comforts. The interior was so vast that two or even three occupants housed in separate quarters need only meet one another over the dining table or some other planned encounter. The opulent décor that the elderly Knights had arranged (and inherited) seemed more suitable for minor royalty than for a child of the Austen family.

But Edward had grown into his role admirably. Over the years, he had received a multitude of assurances that his decision to transfer to the Knight family (and forsake the Austen name) was the correct one. He wore his new ownership like a well-fitted suit, and as he showed Cassie and me to our room, he was no less an object of curiosity to me than his great estate. He ushered us into a room fit for visiting dignitaries.

Edward beamed, "Will this do?"

"It will do for Cassie. Where is my room?" I demanded.

Cassie shook her head. "I am afraid, Edward, you may have become unused to Jane's manners."

"I do have some memory of them," he smiled indulgently.

"My manners are of no consequence," I interjected. "Edward must mind *his* manners and introduce me to all his friends. The young, handsome, clever ones. The old, red-faced bores you may refer to Cassie."

Edward stifled a smile. "And now my memory is fully restored. Jane, we have many entertainments planned. I think you shall meet your fill of new acquaintance."

Oh, the possibility. The glittering promise of imminent happiness. I flung myself onto the bed, bouncing up and down in gleeful anticipation.

The next day was spent primarily in the company of my nieces and nephews; so much more relaxing than the company of adults. They were strong and healthy and I delighted in their growing minds. And I took the responsibilities of aunthood very seriously. When I was wanted, I was at their disposal. And so I was led through a gauntlet of their favorite games and hiding places. We wandered the far edge of the grounds to the livestock area, where I was greeted by the sight of improbably clean pigs, going in and out of a gothically inspired animal house.

"Even the pigs are distinguished," I noted.

The children had wisely anticipated that only I, of all their guests, could appreciate such a sight.

◇◇◇

Two days later, the house filled up still further with more guests; four gentlemen and two ladies from Elizabeth's family arrived. It was no random visit, for Edward and Elizabeth were to throw their first major ball in four day's time. Yes, our own visit was most well-timed.

That evening, we sat down to a dinner party of fifteen. The food was delicious and two of our new additions were very handsome unmarried men! It was too public a forum to fully make their acquaintance (certainly not under my mother's and Elizabeth's watchful eyes). But the near future promised great opportunities, and I was content.

Afterward, the ladies and gentlemen retired to their respective drawing rooms. Edward stood at our door to bid us goodnight. I waved him away.

"Go on, Edward. We know that the company of ladies is nothing to the stench of a good cigar."

He acknowledged, "I do have to attend to the ..."

"Debauchery," I offered helpfully.

"...*well-being* of our male guests. Ladies ..."

As he exited, I took note that the ladies seemed rather unnerved by my familiarity. Did none of them have brothers?

Mama had retired early with a headache. Our group included Cassie, Elizabeth, her married sister Margaret, and their young cousin Lady Sarah Edmonton, a twenty year old heiress. The conversation quickly came to revolve around Sarah's matrimonial prospects, and I listened with keen interest. Sarah had already eliminated one suitor, a Lord Winchell, from consideration because, while he had a fine Devon estate, his house in town was "frightfully small." So small that she could never receive guests there. But Lord Winchell's defects did not end there. He wearied her when he prattled on about war or investments.

"It is well that he respects your comprehension and judgment on such matters," I offered.

Sarah shrugged distastefully. "I much prefer a man who loves to hunt and takes an interest in fashion."

I exchanged a look with Cassie. The cause and effect sequence of wealth and feeblemindedness never ceased to fascinate me. Was it unjust coincidence that such a shallow and inferior mind be blessed with such wealth? Or was it wealth that insulated the mind from being challenged and stimulated to a full healthy growth? If Sarah's gifts had to be taken as a whole, I could not envy her. Elizabeth, however, remained an admirer.

Elizabeth chimed in, "I am most anxious to acquaint you with Lord Benchley. His house in town will certainly not disappoint. Magnificent ballroom, and such a collection of paintings … particularly in the library."

"He does not spend all his time reading, does he?" Sarah whined.

"He is a handsome and charming man," Elizabeth wheedled.

He may not have aroused Sarah's interest, but *I* was certainly anxious to meet him.

"He sounds a most welcome addition to the ball. I look forward to making his acquaintance," I enthused.

Now it was time for Elizabeth and Margaret to exchange looks. Margaret could not hold back a smug, condescending smile.

"Of course, my dear. I'm sure he ... and his family will consider themselves most fortunate for the chance of your company. Your charms are not to be resisted."

And there it was. It was not only that they wanted to reserve Sarah's prerogative to choose Lord Benchley, but that it was considered ludicrous that I could ever consider myself a fit match for him. There appeared to be such a clear unspoken consensus on the matter that I was made aware that my marital prospects had already been the subject of discussion and amusement. For while I was setting my sights on the goal of a wealthy man, I entirely forgot to take into account the small matter of family. It was with this newfound awareness that I sat and wrote in bed that night to anchor my story with the weight of reality.

Mrs. Fanny Dashwood, a handsome woman of forty years stood beside young Miss Lucy Steele along a treacherously steep hill with beautiful views. Lucy looked entreatingly at the older woman.

"I have been secretly engaged for five years. But you are the first person with whom I've dared to share this secret," young Lucy confided.

Mrs. Dashwood was both surprised and pleased. "My dear, why such concern? Do you see objections from his family?"

"Their disapproval is my greatest fear. For as you know, I have nothing. No dowry, no inheritance."

"You will overcome all resistance the

moment they meet you," Mrs Dashwood
soothed. "You charms are not to be
resisted."

"Oh, if only it were so," Lucy sighed.

"You will be welcomed with open arms.
I haven't the slightest doubt."

Lucy smiled gratefully. "It is your
brother. Edward. You and I are to be sisters,
my dear Fanny."

Lucy opened her arms wide to receive
Mrs. Dashwood's embrace. Mrs. Dashwood
moved quickly towards Lucy. Not with a
hug, though, but a shove! Lucy's shrill
scream faded as her body plummeted down
the canyon. Mrs. Dashwood's eyes blazed
dark and narrow with fury (never to be
visited by remorse.) She wanted to thrash
her brother for bringing their family so
close to the brink of this degradation. But
this satisfaction was not to be possible, as it
was going to be necessary to distance
herself from clumsy Lucy's unfortunate
mishap.

Although I was pleased with this addition, it was
perhaps the sight of Cassie sleeping beside me that brought
me to understand that while its harshness might delight a
group of young boys, its violence should probably be
moderated to suit a more mature audience.

"It is your brother. Edward. You and I
are to be sisters, my dear Fanny," Lucy

confided.

Mrs. Dashwood's face contorted with rage. Alarmed, Lucy wisely stepped away from the cliff.

Better. Just a hint of violent intention. It was enough to content and lull me to sleep.

In the morning, I bundled up, wandered the gardens, and settled down with a book at the base of a statue. I had momentarily had my fill of company. Nonetheless, my father's approach was still most welcome.

"Does the cold weather enhance your reading?" he inquired.

"Only biographies and cookbooks. Fiction requires a warm room," I replied.

"And what of letters?"

He handed me one, dirty and water-damaged, but still a miraculous sight. It was from Frank! I leapt to my feet. But even reading it demanded more patience than I could muster.

"Frank? He is well?"

"Tolerably," Papa smiled.

"Any excuse for his unpardonable tardiness?"

"He did have a nasty bout of influenza. He appears to be back on his feet, though," Papa explained.

"Influenza! I could *throttle* him."

I flung myself into my father's arms, ecstatic with relief. The last several weeks had been a torturous exercise in pushing thoughts of Frank and the Naval mutiny to the far edge of my thoughts. For when I dwelt upon them, I sank into a debilitating state that deprived me of the ability to do so much as lift as arm. And all for naught! Frank alive and well. At least, well enough for my peace of mind. The influenza was, in all likelihood, long behind him. Unburdened, my mind was free to focus on the task at hand, and to revel at the prospect of the impending ball. Now, I could fling myself into it with full enjoyment. The night before the ball, I slept more peacefully than I had since childhood.

The ballroom was a most impressive spectacle. The guests must have numbered over three hundred. All landed gentry and aristocracy from within a hundred miles were present. And no small number had braved the trip from town just for the occasion. There was a small smattering of professionals and Army officers. The evening was young, but I was already impatient for my introductions. I watched from a distance with Cassie as our visiting young heiress was swarmed by a bevy of admirers.

"They have talked to her long enough to uncover her deficiencies. Oh, where is Edward? He shirks his duties," I groused.

"And what duties are those?"

"Matrimonial assistance. Of course, I could always introduce myself."

I knew this suggestion was bound to invoke Cassie's horror.

"Yes, I know. We would then be obliged to change our name and move to the West Indies," I continued.

Contrary to my threats, I was all too aware of protocol

and the dictates of polite society. This was, in fact, one of my chief arguments against a life in Bath. The correct way to dress and the correct way to behave were enforced to the point of suffocating exhaustion. Formal society was like a pair of tight shoes that could be uncomfortably endured for one evening, but would drive one to mad distraction for any serious length of time. And so, for one evening at the Godmersham ball, I was cheerfully resigned to a night of good behavior. But undoing my good intentions was the sight of Sarah and her unwarranted popularity. As if to underscore the point, Elizabeth's sister Margaret joined us.

"Cassandra. Jane. I do hope you're enjoying the ball."

"Very much," Cassie assured her.

"And Sarah appears to be having a marvelous time, which certainly puts *my* mind at ease," I added, hoping she would take my meaning.

"Lord Benchley has arrived and longs to make Sarah's acquaintance. Though I hate to disappoint her new friends."

Just the assignment I required. "Allow me."

I marched across the dance floor, secured an introduction to Sarah's audience, and dispatched her off in the direction of her cousin.

"I trust you are enjoying your stay at Godmersham," one gentleman offered.

"Edward and Elizabeth have been most kind," I responded.

"The pleasure of your visit has been heightened, I trust, by the company of Lady Sarah?"

"She is such a lovely girl," a second gentleman added.

"I have long heard her beauty and charm admired, and am happy to finally enjoy them myself," a third admirer chimed in.

I did my utmost to contain my reaction. "Indeed, her beauty is overshadowed only by her quality of mind."

The gentlemen all nodded enthusiastic assent. It strained all belief. Did they only mean to be polite, with those effusions of admiration? I feared worse; I feared they were in earnest. It was insufferable. Before I had time to fabricate a means of excusing myself, Edward came to my rescue. But it was a rescue of very mixed blessings, as he was accompanied by Mr. Tucker, a portly man of sixty years, who immediately asked me to join him on the dance floor.

I had little choice but to accept his arm and pray that my grimace resembled a smile. In passing, I caught Edward's eye and tried to convey my extreme displeasure. Mr. Tucker was but the first of many similar dance partners, all middle-aged, heavy, and balding. And thus employed, I was continually treated to glimpses of Sarah all evening long, in the arms of the room's handsomest bachelors.

At one time, my dance took me in the vicinity of a spirited conversation regarding the Navy. I strained to hear.

"Men who have been in the Navy for over ten years have such cracked and weather-beaten skin. They are frightful to look upon," one man expounded. "But my chief objection is this: it brings individuals of obscure birth into undue distinction."

Another gentleman put his hand on the speaker's shoulder to silence him, and glanced furtively in my direction. I did not know him but clearly he knew me. Or at least all he needed to know. That I was Edward's sister. A lowly Austen. With two brothers in the same military so soundly abused by his companion. That their honoured host had a multitude of embarrassing connections, that for his sake, must quietly be endured by the rest of polite society.

I was not introduced to a single unmarried man for the whole of the evening. When I caught my brother's eye on the ballroom floor, he looked away quickly, ashamed. Perhaps Elizabeth had indoctrinated him the previous evening. Or perhaps he could simply see with his own eyes. Clearly, he regretted encouraging my hopes. The night I had looked forward to with such anticipation, could not end soon enough. The oblivion of sleep was my only salvation.

It was a chilly spring afternoon the next day, but the gardens seemed vastly preferable to Godmersham's stifling interior. But even there, relief was not to be found, as I spied Lady Sarah at a distance, strolling the grounds with one of her new admirers. Was her high pitched shrieking laughter music to his ears? I nearly ran back into the estate, but I was unwilling to encounter my family, against whom I was fast developing an unforgiving resentment. It was my dear family I had to blame for my pathetic miscalculations. They, who admired my opinions, my stories, my beauty. Oh, naturally, I had assumed that I would amuse and delight and secure the affections of the whole world just as easily. They ruined me. They deceived me. Why did they not warn me that it is the bank that determines human value? That in the eyes of society, I am worth nothing. Then I could have been spared the agony of the previous night. The better I understand the workings of the world, the less it can injure me.

And so I braved any unwelcome encounters and marched back to the house, straight to my "finished" manuscript. Elinor and Marianne Dashwood required a harsher fate.

> *Marianne Dashwood lay ill and motionless. Elinor hovered anxiously. The doctor leaned over Marianne and took her pulse.*
>
> *"I am very sorry to tell you this, Miss Dashwood. Your sister is dead," the doctor pronounced sadly.*
>
> *In an instant, Marianne's eyes flew open, and she and Elinor, both turned angrily to the incompetent doctor, who stammered with embarrassment.*
>
> *"No, no. Of course she's not DEAD. She must live, mustn't she? She must live and she must suffer."*
>
> *Elinor and Marianne received the prognosis with equal measures of resignation and fury.*

Now I was able to write "THE END" with a flourish, and a great deal of morbid satisfaction.

It was time for a walk into town. At three miles distance, it would consume at least four hours, and I badly wanted for time to disappear as quickly as possible. I had desire for neither company nor a carriage, which Edward would gladly have provided. My mother would not have approved the solitary excursion. She would worry about the townspeople whispering about why a guest at Godmersham should tramp about the countryside on foot. But I was not feeling kindly disposed towards my family as a whole and would not trouble myself to uphold their reputation.

The beauty of the countryside was insufficient to lighten my dark mood. The weather was fine … too fine, in fact. Ominous black clouds and a raging storm would have suited me better. Could it be only yesterday that I was filled with such childish and pathetic expectation for a triumphant union? It felt most unfair to be caught unawares at this time of life. If only it had been explained to me from an early age … my lack of value in the marriage economy. Then I should be quite reconciled by now to a long, unending, solitary future.

It was in this foul mood that I set my foot into a well hidden rabbit hole, and tumbled immediately to the ground, crying out at the sharp spasm of pain emanating from my left ankle and from the shock of the fall. Why, oh why had I chosen not to walk on the road, but two hundred yards distant? Of course I had not wanted my solitary gloom disturbed by encountering another soul and all the requisite social courtesies involved. But my unsociable decision had put me out of the path of assistance. I was still half a mile short of town, and two and a half away from Godmersham. How long does it take to crawl two and a half miles? Would I be out here all night? How long would it take a search party to find me? Why had I not eaten a heartier breakfast?

I was so consumed with these alarming speculations that I failed to notice a tall figure of a man striding with determination in my direction, until he was almost upon me. What a relief! So few things to be thankful for, but at least I was not completely forsaken. Hmm. A Naval uniform. But what was this! His right arm was tightly bandaged and secured in a sling. For Heaven's Sake! In my hurried prayers, had I *failed* to specify an able-bodied rescuer?

"Madam, I witnessed your fall as I was returning to

town. Please allow me to be of assistance."

I nodded consent. "It is my ankle."

He used his free hand to check for broken bones. Having a closer look at him, I could tell from his sunburnt skin that he had been at sea recently. He had intelligent features, perhaps even well-favoured. For the moment, they were etched with concern.

"Just a sprain, but you won't be able to walk on it. Use your right foot and let me help you up."

Somehow, between my bad foot and his bad arm, I was standing upright, precariously clutching his left arm to maintain my balance.

"I have to get back to Godmersham," I informed him.

"Godmersham! Am I to take it then that you are Lady Sarah Edmonton?"

Was there no escaping the insipid Lady Sarah?

"I am sorry to disappoint," I glowered.

His head tucked in an apologetic bow. "I beg your pardon. I had only heard something of her visit. But it is of no consequence. At any rate, I am very happy to see you safely home. But we must go to town first. It is but fifteen minutes."

"I cannot limp any distance on one foot. Here is what you must do. Go to Godmersham. They will send a carriage for me, and you can direct them to my location. I shall rest here."

"Leave you alone here! For two hours or more! Madam, I would no more abandon you than a fallen comrade."

"But I cannot walk."

"Then I shall carry you."

"Your arm will not allow it."

"But my left shoulder is fit enough."

And with that, he bent down and unceremoniously flung me over his shoulder. I dangled there in mortified outrage.

"How dare you! Put me down at once."

"I am terribly sorry, but this is the one true option available to us. Now please be calm, and this ordeal will be of short duration."

"Lieutenant ...?"

"Barnes. It is Lieutenant Barnes. How did you know I was a lieutenant?"

"It is on your uniform as clear as day," I snapped.

"Yes, but few young ladies know the insignia, Miss ...?"

"Austen. Miss Jane Austen. I am the sister of Mr. Edward Knight, who has just taken possession of the Godmersham estate. You cannot propose to carry me into town, over your shoulder, like a sack of potatoes."

"We are a nation at war, Miss Austen. Worse indignities have been suffered, I assure you."

His tone quieted me; but my cheeks still burned at the prospect of our entry into the crowded streets below. I really must cease to dwell on the fact that my life cannot get any worse, because I am proven wrong every time.

I will endeavor my utmost to forget ensuing events. The pointing of fingers and the laughter were much as anticipated. Then when I closed my eyes to block it all out, how many louts ran and inquired, "Is she dead then?" and backed away from the most withering glare I could muster. But at least my agenda had been decided. Last night's humiliation might not have justified fleeing the county, but this afternoon's disgrace sealed the necessity. Papa will listen to reason. He must. Surely after these last punishing years ... Tom Lefroy, and being banished from our own home, the money troubles, the months of anxiety over Frank, and now these recent events, and the disagreeable prospect of Bath ... surely I was as deserving of a respite as any soul could be. Well, perhaps deserving is not the right word. But in *need* of a respite, without question, or I should break down in complete hysteria.

Lieutenant Barnes secured a wagon, and I had but another hour to suffer his company before I was resting safely in a large drawing room at Godmersham. Unfortunately, he remained far too long, detained by Cassie's gratitude. They chatted earnestly at some distance, while Mama bustled unhelpfully about my bandaged foot.

"You brought this upon yourself, you know. Not asking for a carriage! Well, you were luckier than you deserved to be. Certainly lucky that you were able to avoid any ruffians."

"Not entirely," I muttered in the direction of the irritating Lieutenant Barnes.

"You were also most fortunate that the lieutenant was not going by so quickly in his wagon that he did not see you."

I thought it best that Mama not know that the lieutenant was in fact on foot when he spotted me, and had had closer proximity to my body than any man alive. No, only Cassie would be subjected to the sordid details and I should scold her for gushing over his checkered assistance.

My mother continued, "Your father and I have been thinking that perhaps another week here at Godmersham will do. And that it might be nice to get a little sea air before we are finally settled in Bath. Your father has had invitations from old friends in Lyme, Sidmouth, and Teignmouth as well. Any one of them will do, I'm sure. You and Cassandra will enjoy yourselves."

Oh, rescued again, for the second time in one day, and this time, unequivocally. My mind had been racing with arguments, counter appeals, threats, sulks and all manner of strategy to convince my parents that a departure from Godmersham was imperative. And here, a gift from the heavens had just fallen into my lap, and wonderfully wrapped. I did so greatly enjoy the sea, and could never have devised a better scheme.

At last, the lieutenant was dispatched, with as much feigned gratitude as I could muster. Cassie settled next to me.

"You must tell me all about your mishap," she prodded.

"Later," I said firmly, with a glance in Mama's direction. "Right now, I should like to dream of a holiday in Lyme."

Cassie shook her head thoughtfully. "If there is a choice to be made, I think we should be better off in choosing Sidmouth. I have heard it greatly praised."

"By whom?" I inquired.

Cassie's head turned away as she suddenly busied herself with a piece of needlework nearby.

"Generally ... generally praised."

Mama nodded amenably, and Cassie, as a rule, was so lacking in guile, that I could only shrug my own assent.

"Sidmouth it is ... at once."

Cassie let out an inexplicable sigh of relief. My suspicions should have been aroused. Instead, I could only think, poor Cassie. She asks for so little of life. How nice that we will do something that will give her so much pleasure. That is the trouble with having such a virtuous sister. I was doomed to be caught unawares if her mind should ever turn in a truly devious direction.

CHAPTER FIVE
THE SEA

The sea sparkles and winks and crashes and roars with its immortality. No wonder the Greeks thought there were gods below. How soothing it all was: the sounds, the smell, the breeze, the messiness, and the informality it insisted upon. Why could this not have been our final home, instead of stuffy Bath? Why indeed! My parents would not lose their preoccupation with marrying off their daughters when it was obvious to anyone with half an eye that Cassie had long ago surrendered to her spinster fate and I had recently resolved to join her.

There is freedom in that white flag. To ignore the demands of fashionable society and the weary burden of pleasing. As I no longer needed to make a good impression on anyone outside of my existing circle. I was free to speak and behave in a manner that answered only to my own inclinations. Which is adequate consolation for the loss of marital prospects. Moreover, never again to know crushing heartache and humiliation. I had arrived at a state of enlightened resignation, and my new resolve and new surroundings suited me to perfection.

Shall I never learn how to swim? Certainly not within the confines of this bathing machine, a small uncovered wooden cabin, hauled some twenty yards into the waves. The walls were not solid, but had sufficient gaps between the boards that allowed for the free flow of water. At present, it housed myself, Cassie, Mama, and two other ladies. It could probably have accommodated three more. Its high walls came up to our shoulders and served their purpose well enough: to protect us from the unseemly view of gentlemen, an aim which I certainly upheld. But why could we not claim an entire beach for women alone? With such privacy, we could swim as naked as nymphs. My companions were not troubled by such fanciful longings. They suffered the bracing waters only as a means to an end.

"They say sea bathing will cure asthma, consumption, even dropsy," one lady asserted.

"Also rheumatism and gout," her friend added.

"I pray it is true," my mother responded earnestly. "For I suffer from illnesses of all kinds. Jane, stop splashing about.

"Mama, are you attempting to blame the movement of the ocean on me?" I marveled.

But nothing could destroy my good humor. The sea's healing powers were already upon me.

Our Sidmouth host was a Mr. Shaw, who was nearly my father's age. I believe he was the younger brother of one of Papa's former Oxford cohorts. He was a widower and his children had long scattered to the winds, though he was frequently visited by their missives. Given our family of four and our intended stay of three weeks, we should have felt ourselves to be a great imposition, had he not evidenced such keen delight in having a full house. What luck, for it promised to serve as a welcome haven in the years to come. Moreover, Mr. Shaw had most conveniently chosen to locate himself not ten minutes walk from the ocean.

Still, it was a small home, and after a sociable breakfast, I longed to roam the town. Cassie and I proposed to walk the promenade, and our parents and Mr. Shaw declined the invitation to join us, as I had hoped they would. But our mother fretted our lack of a chaperone. Mr. Shaw agreed.

"There are scoundrels about, that is to be sure. Especially those rascals in the cavalry," Mr. Shaw cautioned.

"It is the cavalry that should be afraid of Jane, and not vice versa," my father noted.

I made ready to protest, but instantly realized I had been painted in a most useful fashion. I did not want the elders to insist that we drag a chaperone about, so better they see me as fit for any challenge. And so I was. Five brothers, and a score of my father's male students had equipped me with an arsenal of verbal assault. I felt equal to anything we could possibly encounter.

The beginning of our stroll was pleasant and blessedly uneventful. There was a full crowd milling about us: families, fashionable shoppers, and no small number of holidaymakers. Cassie and I were unremarkable among them, which pleased me no end. And on every side street, a glance to the left revealed a small stretch of glimmering sea.

"Mr. Shaw offers us the warmest of welcomes, but I am already missing Godmersham," Cassie admitted.

"Yes. I shall miss the children, and the wine ... and

Edward. I had once worried that in becoming a Knight, he should also become a stranger. But he is still our brother, despite his good fortunes. And in addition, he serves as a great inspiration to us both. We may be allowed to hope that somewhere out there is some elderly distant relation who will die in a timely fashion and shower us with a completely unexpected inheritance of enormous proportion."

"Come now, Jane, is that really our only hope?"

"Hmmm. More likely, we will fall on the charity of our brothers. Fortunate that Mama gave us so many of them," I mused.

"There is still one other hope," Cassie hinted.

"No, Cassie. Do not say it. Do not think it. I have done you the courtesy of taking you at your word when you say you are done with all thoughts of marriage. You *must* extend the same courtesy to me," I commanded insistently.

"I know your worth, Jane. And I know why you have given up hope. But you cannot stop me from hoping for you. Though for your sake, I will do it in silence."

How exasperating she was, and what a fine sister all the same. We linked arms and surveyed the multitude of possibilities for spending our small allowances.

Some half way down the promenade, I felt Cassie stop in her tracks and tighten her grip around me.

"Jane, dear, do you remember when you sprained your foot at Godmersham, and a Lieutenant Barnes came to your assistance?"

"How could I forget," I scoffed. "That odious man who carried me into town like a sack of flour. Unpardonable, ill-mannered, uncultured, philistine …"

I could not finish my words, for we found ourselves face to face with the philistine himself.

"Lieutenant Barnes, how good to see you again," Cassie managed.

"Miss Austen, what a great pleasure. I am happy to see that you took my recommendation of a holiday in Sidmouth," he replied.

Recommendation! What was this!? Cassie *knew* that he would be here and deliberately arranged for us to be in his path!! While knowing that I never wanted to lay eyes on him for the entirety of my life? I tried to will Cassie to meet my incensed gaze, but she was studiously determined to avoid it. Lieutenant Barnes introduced us to his companion, his younger brother Dr. Andrew Barnes. He was taller than the lieutenant and less sunburnt. Otherwise, the family resemblance was quite apparent. The lieutenant greeted me with the requisite courtesies and inquired as to the health of my foot. I responded through clenched teeth, hoping that he had the smallest amount of discernment necessary to know that I wished him gone. Whether from stupidity or malice, he failed to understand me. Instead, he suggested that the four of us continue our stroll together! Was it but half an hour ago that I felt gratitude for such a caring sister? At that moment, I could have thrown her to the sharks.

We headed towards the ocean, to a smooth path on a small incline above the beach. I hoped the roar of the waves would impede conversation, but Lieutenant Barnes and Cassie were determined to be social. Apparently, the Barnes brothers were staying nearby at their aunt's summer home. She owned an estate in Somerset as well. The lieutenant's broken arm had kept him away from duty for some four weeks now, and he predicted another month until he reached a full recovery.

"Not that long, surely," I argued. "Perhaps if you were

to take that cast off, you will find that you are already mended."

"That is a tempting hypothesis. What says my doctor to such an experiment?" he responded, with a sidelong wink at his brother.

"Your doctor says no. Now, while I will allow you to have a superior mind, your bones are of tediously average strength, and will heal at their leisure," Dr. Barnes asserted.

Lieutenant Barnes shrugged. "It seems as if I will be here for the duration of your holiday, Miss Jane."

"Even so, I will pray nightly to hasten the date of your healthy departure."

Cassie bumped into me to caution me on my manners, but now it was my turn to ignore *her*. As our walk continued, we came across a young woman of about sixteen years of age, running up a steep stairwell that connected the beach and our path. She easily slipped under the side railing, and would continually leap down the side of the stairwell from increasingly higher levels, causing considerable alarm for her companions.

"Perhaps we ought to give her a word of warning," Dr. Barnes mused.

"Do not trouble yourself," I argued. "A girl that foolish should not live long enough to breed."

The Barnes brothers exchanged a look of astonishment, and Cassie was gratifyingly mortified.

I continued, "For the world can easily do without the eight or ten children whose character has been molded by her stupid and ignorant influence."

Cassie stepped forward. "Oh dear, the tide! The tide! It is remarkable how far it comes in this late in the day," she noted loudly.

Her attempt to distract the gentlemen was far from successful. I felt the Lieutenant examine me at great length. At the same time, his brother quickly remembered an obligation that required that we excuse them to leave. Success, at last! But just as we had returned to the bustling street, and we were almost free of them, Cassie lost all good sense.

"We have never been able to really thank you for your kindness to Jane. I believe my parents have fixed plans for tomorrow. But can you join us for tea, the day after?"

Lieutenant Barnes accepted graciously, taking care to observe my reaction. I was livid, but would not give him the satisfaction of seeing me vexed. For what else could be his goal in persisting after our company, when I had made it so plain that I disliked him. And I was certain that he disliked me as well.

After the gentlemen departed, I fumed, "I wonder what he *means* by being so civil?"

"It is a natural talent for some. You certainly did your best to secure his dislike," Cassie chided.

"That was the whole of my scheme," I explained impatiently. "If they find me disagreeable, we shall not be obliged to spend further time in their company. Why on earth did you invite them to tea?"

Cassie's feeble excuses fell on deaf ears. I was going to have to apply my full imagination if I were to evade this appointment. How sad I had no other acquaintance in Sidmouth that could necessitate a regretful collision of plans. Perhaps I could be laid up in bed with some imaginary illness. Mama did it often enough. Yet, to be convincingly indisposed would require keeping up the ruse at least the entire day ... losing a full precious day of sunshine, gulls squawking, and salty coastal breezes. No, our days here were numbered and Lieutenant Frederick Barnes would not be allowed to deprive me of my daily measure of enjoyment.

That evening, I retired to a corner of the parlour as Papa and Mr. Shaw continued their reminiscences and Cassie and Mama tended to a pile of mending. My mind required occupation, and since I had shut the door on *Elinor and Marianne* and their sad conclusion, it was time to commence the next story. I had no clear idea of the hero or heroine, but I was happy to begin my tale with a portrait of the villain, whose objectionable character was immediately apparent to all, even on first acquaintance.

The proud, haughty Mr. Darcy stepped out of his carriage and was greeted with the unwholesome sight of a stray dog relieving himself against one of the carriage wheels. Darcy summoned his manservant, who had been employed unloading luggage onto the sidewalk.

"Do you see that dog there?" Darcy demanded.

"Yes, sir," his servant replied.

"Well, you should have seen him earlier. You are dismissed."

His servant stammered uncomprehendingly.

"Did you finish unloading the trunks?" Mr. Darcy inquired coldly.

"Not quite, sir."

"Well, before you leave my employ, finish unloading, find me a porter ... and

shoot the dog."

The man knew better than to argue. "Very good, sir."

Mr. Darcy examined the results of his most recent manicure and waited impatiently.

There. The one constant advantage of dealing with disagreeable people was that they helped to populate my stories in vivid, albeit well-disguised fashion. In fact, I could remember occasions where I welcomed the encounter with a ridiculous, prideful, or narrow-minded character. They made for great sport, entertaining letters, and satisfying literary fodder. Thus, I would reconcile myself to the teeth-grinding prospect of a tea with Lieutenant Barnes. But on pain of death, I would procure Cassie's word that no further invitations would be extended.

The next day I had envisioned as a peaceful day of reprieve. But why hope for such a unicorn? Did each day not guarantee a fresh set of trials and unwelcome developments? Hmph! Or did that only ring true for myself. For *someone* out there *must* be leading a charmed existence.

I was to be incarcerated at another family obligation: the entertainment of Reverend Samuel Blackall, five and thirty years of age. He had entered our lives via an introduction from Mrs. Anne Lefroy. The same Mrs. Lefroy who was aunt to Tom Lefroy, the first and only man I would ever allow to catch my heart so unawares. I knew that my heartache had weighed upon her. And she was as determined as my parents to see me happily married. To that end, Reverend Blackall had been submitted as a candidate, and a peace offering.

In principle, I appreciated her efforts. And as my father had been a clergyman, I certainly could have no objection to the profession. Indeed, I looked upon it quite favorably. But Reverend Blackall! He was a cliché of pomp and self-importance. A man who welcomed every opportunity to present himself. Though his profession dictated a somber and modest attire, I think he should have been delighted if his position imposed more fashionable obligations.

"It was Madame Lefroy who introduced me to my patroness, Lady Eugenia Winthrop," Reverend Blackall rhapsodized.

"It must be rather daunting to be in such fine company," my mother prattled.

"Not at all. I consider the clerical office as equal in point of dignity with the highest rank of the kingdom. And I do possess the gift of pleasing her ladyship with such compliments and flattery befitting one of her exalted station."

"And do these compliments spring from the moment?" I inquired. "Or are they the work of previous rehearsal?"

"Jane!" my mother admonished.

But she need not have worried. Reverend Blackall's mind could not comprehend criticism or being laughed at, and thus he interpreted all comments as admiration. He was certain that we listened with gratifying enthrallment as he explained that whenever he had an odd ten or fifteen minutes to fill in his day, he would try to compose a universally applicable flattery that could quickly be recited when a convenient moment arose.

But as he sought to impress, and as my parents attempted to induce a romantic intrigue, I could only watch the scheme unfold with amazement; such an exquisite mixture of folly would certainly find its way into my latest story.

Later that night in our room, Cassie took me to task once more for my deplorable manners.

"I was as civil to him as his bad breath would allow," I defended.

"As a courtesy to Madame Lefroy ..." Cassie wheedled.

"She seeks to make amends. For depriving me of a clever, handsome, young man, she sends me a pretentious middle-aged goat to take his place."

"Put your writing away and get some rest," Cassie commanded.

"Oh, no. First you inflict the evil lieutenant on me. And now the incomparable Reverend Blackall. No, I must write to Martha and beg that her presence is urgently required."

Cassie sighed and watched me pen a heated testimony of distress to our dear friend, sparing her none of my recent sufferings. Clearly it was time to gather allies about me. Sadly, Martha would not be in time for tomorrow's ordeal. I tossed and turned in bed that night. The warm bedroom failed to catch the cool breezes outside. And the prospect of seeing the lieutenant for tea did not make for peaceful dreams.

It was after one o'clock in the morning when I climbed out of bed, pulled back the curtains for moonlight, and began to dress. The rustling awoke Cassie. I told her to return to sleep, but that the warm air was too much for me. If I could only steal down to the waves, and feel the cool water wash over my ankles, I should cool down immediately.

"You cannot be serious. To go down to the beach? At this hour?" Cassie inquired in disbelief.

"Go back to sleep. I shall return very shortly."

Of course, she did not return to sleep. She scrambled out of her bed and into her clothes, fussing at me all the while. And she quietly followed me out of the house and down to the beach ... as I fully intended for her to do.

Thank goodness Mr. Shaw's house was situated so close to the water. The night air had such a cooling effect, that immersion in the water could no longer exactly be regarded as a necessity. But this was no time for half measures. The waves beckoned and the full moon revealed a deserted landscape. What unparalleled opportunity; we were utterly alone! I made haste to pull my clothes off, amidst Cassie's horrified protests.

"Jane! Jane! You were only to dip your ankles in. Have you gone mad?" she pleaded.

"Tonight, the sea belongs to you and me alone, Cassie. But we must take advantage, for this circumstance will *never* come again."

I ran into the waves, my loud squeals buried by the roar of the waves. It was an extraordinary peak of sensation. The cold water was exhilarating, but the freedom was an even more potent drug.

"Jane, you must not go so far in. You could drown."

"And when I do, the entire family will wonder why you did not trouble yourself to pull me to safety," I goaded.

To underscore my words, I allowed the next incoming wave to knock me to my knees. By the time I righted myself, I was rewarded with a view of my alarmed sister scrambling out of her dress. I greeted her pained, cautious entry with a series of drenching splashes. Which of course, she could only answer with frantic retaliation. Her screams and laughter were even louder than mine. It was such a fine and keen moment of experience; I knew the memory would be with us for years to come. And never had the advantages of spinsterhood been so fully apparent. For what husband would have allowed such activities? That night, we floated in the waters of freedom and contentment. And envied no one.

CHAPTER SIX
DREADFUL SUITORS

My spirits were fully rejuvenated the next day as we awaited the arrival of the lieutenant and his brother. The giddiness of our moonlight adventures could overpower any discomfort or annoyance that the lieutenant could inflict.

Our guests arrived amidst a flurry of introductions and pleasantries. The medical expertise of Dr. Barnes provided a great fascination for his elderly hosts: a future resource for the daily aches and pains of advanced years. He was normally situated in Portsmouth, tending primarily to naval casualties, and had only stolen away for the occasion of his brother's convalescence.

Cassie had just left the room to get water and refreshments when an innocent commentary from Mr. Shaw on the fine weather and full moon of the previous night turned the conversation down an alarming path.

"Astronomy is a great passion with me and the stars were magnificent last night," the lieutenant enthused.

"You have a telescope, then?" my father inquired.

"A very powerful one," he replied.

His brother confessed that while he had some small interest in the stars, it was not sufficiently strong to keep himself awake until two o'clock in the morning, no matter how often the lieutenant had requested his company.

"No matter. I had all the company I needed last night," the lieutenant announced mysteriously.

"Well, I know we cannot suspect Aunt Doherty. So where did you obtain company at that hour of the night?" Dr. Barnes challenged.

"As it happens, I chanced to cast my lens over to the ocean. And I was rewarded by the sight of two of the most beautiful seals I have ever seen. Playing delightfully on the beach."

He looked me straight in the eye and added, "Females, I believe."

Mr. Shaw marveled, "You could tell at that distance?? That *is* a wondrous lens."

No. No. No. No. No. No. No. It cannot be. I refused to believe it. I had done nothing so terrible in life that I should be thus punished. It was a misunderstanding, surely. A concoction of my overheated imagination. He certainly must be referring to the sight of two actual seals, and not two naked sisters who were frolicking in complete, total, absolute, and utter privacy. Heinous villain! The little smile lingering on the corner of his lips left no hope, but pointed to the bleakest interpretation. Oh, no. I am ever armed to do battle, but … what of my poor sister?

"Pray, do not mention this incident to Cassandra, as she is exceedingly fearful of seals, and the very mention of them would induce a trauma," I warned threateningly.

"Dear, dear," Mr. Shaw worried.

I continued, "All earthly and heavenly justice would demand the most unimaginable punishment to anyone who would purposely upset as dear a soul as our Cassie."

"Jane!" my mother admonished.

Lieutenant Barnes soothed, "Ma'am, you are assured of my silence."

Whereupon Cassie rejoined us and great efforts were made by all to redirect the conversation into safe and mundane territories. Another half hour and Mr. Shaw was obliged to excuse himself, for he had a regularly scheduled walk with his friend Mr. Maxwell every afternoon.

"Perhaps we shall see those seals along the beach," he mused.

Then he remembered himself, and patted Cassie on the shoulder with a penitent sigh. "I'm so sorry, my dear. I quite forgot."

Cassie was of course, in confusion, and the evil lieutenant unsuccessfully tried to smother his amusement. The afternoon could not end quickly enough.

Outside the cottage, when the hour of deliverance had finally arrived, I was newly aggrieved to see Cassie and Lieutenant Barnes pull away into a tête-à-tête at some distance from the rest of us. If she dared to invite him into our home again, I should have to advertise for a new sister. Dr. Barnes shared my suspicions, but not my sentiments. He in fact hinted that he suspected the pair were forming an attachment. After all, had they not conspired to be in Sidmouth at the same time? It was a coupling of which he heartily approved. As the doctor sang Cassie's praises, I could hardly contain myself.

Sly, deceitful sister! She had promised to be my greatest comfort and now thought to bring a fiend into my life, for all of eternity. How could she even consider it? That was to say, I had certainly been urging her for some years now to set her grief aside and to find another worthy matrimonial prospect. I had wished for it so dearly, for her sake. Because she deserved true happiness. And as I gazed at her from a distance, I could not deny that she appeared to be in remarkable spirits. How could he possibly suit her? And even if he did, it was a requirement of anyone who attached himself to my Cassie that he suited *me* as well. In this particular case, my approval could never be extended. Would she please stop smiling? This was awful.

Perhaps my Mama's complaints were not simply of her imagination, for a litany of them descended on me at once: stomach ache, heart palpitations, shortness of breath, and a pounding of the skull. It was enough to excuse myself from this disturbing scene, and retire to the comfort of my bed. Not to sleep, but to examine my heart. When I still held onto my girlhood fantasies of marriage, I could not bear the thought of leaving Cassie behind; she must marry as well. Now that I was reconciled to an unwedded existence, I had anticipated that Cassie would be at my side for the whole of my life. And who could ask for a better companion? But why had she not arrived at the same conclusion concerning me!?

The next few days were without incident until … my mother joined Cassie and me on our daily excursion. We each of us had such a list of errands and acquisitions to make that three hours soon passed and we were in need of refreshment. A window display of marzipans and tasty puddings drew us into a large café for afternoon tea.

"When is Martha Lloyd to arrive?" my mother inquired.

"She will be here very shortly and is staying in a house not twenty minutes away. We shall be very glad of her company," I replied.

"Well, until then, here is company that we can be very glad of indeed. Reverend Blackall! How good to see you," Mama greeted him excitedly.

Dear Lord. What troublesome men populated this town! Reverend Blackall was determined to secure an invitation to our party, and my mother happily obliged. He inquired as to our business in town, and we summarized the mundane details with appropriate brevity. But I should have known that he would not be able to do the same. We were treated to an extensive discourse on his search for the perfect letter wax and the difficulty of deciding between the multitude of shoelace varieties, for not only must a clergyman provide a model of grooming for his parish, but he must also be handsomely attired to honor the numerous social invitations that his patroness Lady Eugenia Winthrop had bestowed upon him. The mention of this lady brought forth a seemingly unending tribute to her fine qualities and extraordinary abode.

"I am sure it is difficult for you to envision, but her estate has ninety-six windows! Can you imagine the immensity of the building? It is more like a castle than anything else. And there are a full sixteen fireplaces. I am sure you would be very excited at the prospect of seeing such a marvelous sight," the Reverend enthused, looking at me expectantly.

Well, I had seen many a fireplace in my life, and while I was grateful for their warmth, I had never regarded them as a visiting attraction. Why should I be subjected to the tedious details of Lady Winthrop's windows and carpets and servants and china? I would just as soon hear Mama drone on about the state of her bowels.

"In comparison, my own home is rather humble, but quite spacious and comfortable for a small family. Indeed, Lady Winthrop has been most helpful with suggestions on arrangements and decorations, all to help get the home in readiness for its future mistress. She will be a fortunate woman, I assure you, for I am certain most young ladies would feel blessed for the connections and security I can confer on her, owing to my happy situation."

I had until that moment been paying as little attention as possible, but I could not help but feel the burning gazes of both the Reverend and Mama upon me. Their intents were so transparent and so preposterous, I nearly broke out in uncontrollable laughter. Thankfully, I was able to divert it into a coughing fit, and Cassie aided my cause with a few violent thumps to my back. What an entertainingly silly man. He so worshipped titles and enormous houses. I did not mind either, so long as they were peopled with kind hearts and sensible minds. As for Reverend Blackall, every shoe must have its partner, and no doubt there was a silly woman somewhere out there who loved nothing better than circling the perimeter of large estates and counting their windows.

Oh, but look at that hopeful gleam in Mama's eyes. I should not wait long to disabuse her of this ridiculous fantasy. It was an argument that I rather looked forward to, for it would give me occasion to recount a multitude of evidence regarding the Reverend's amusingly shallow qualities. Even Mama should be at loss for rebuttal.

Nonetheless, I knew she would bemoan my lack of good sense and practicality. What young lady turns down such opportunities for security? Mama's interests and mine have often been at odds. In this case, she must lose a son-in-law, or I must marry the unworthiest of prospects. Here, I held an unparalleled guarantee of victory. In this matter, if no other, I owned the power of refusal. If I chose spinsterhood over Reverend Blackall, no one could compel me to do otherwise. I was thus able to peacefully endure the remainder of our tea, and try to busy my mind with thoughts of a far more welcome guest.

The day of dear Martha's arrival had finally come, and Cassie and I were in high spirits when we met her carriage.

"Martha, how we have missed you," I embraced her tightly.

"And I have been a pitiful creature, without my dearest friends. How is the family? Are your parents in health?" Martha inquired.

"Very good health," Cassie assured her.

"And your mother?" Martha smiled. "Pray ... how are her bowels?"

"I thank you for your kind inquiries," I responded delightedly. "Her bowels have been the cause of much recent speculation."

"Have there been improvements in frequency?"

"To our great relief, she enjoys a regular healthful frequency. But, there continue to be concerns about ... consistency."

Martha and I burst into peals of laughter, as Cassie quickly surveyed our surroundings to make sure we were not overheard.

"Wicked girls," she reprimanded.

But it was a hollow complaint. We were never in better spirits than when the three of us were together. Our family holiday was now complete. Unfortunately, Martha did have to be settled away from us, in the home of an old spinster friend of the family, Miss Stent. But Cassie and I arranged to return for a social call that same evening after supper. Our visit was timed both not to impose two additional mouths to feed on Miss Stent's limited resources, but also to coincide with the elderly woman's bedtime: a great opportunity for open and confidential exchanges.

Miss Stent's cottage was filled with considerable clutter; although I was sure she regarded most of these items as treasured keepsakes. And a certain odour in the air that always seemed to signify old age. Poor Martha. She was four and thirty and did not need such a bleak reminder of the solitude and poverty that lay ahead.

Miss Stent herself was the absolute picture of spinsterhood perfected. And I feared that she regarded the three of us as her protégée whom she could happily lend a guiding hand. She shared some specifics of bread and stew recipes that would generate quantity appropriate for a single individual. And she had much to say on the subject of mending clothes, for ladies in "our" circumstances should almost never waste money on new fabric, there no longer being need to impress. My vanity bristled. I should hope I was a good many years from no longer caring about what I look like. Cassie, of course, was attentive and gracious. She shouldered the burden of the evening until Miss Stent was at last ready to retire. Our hostess assured us there were more lessons of economy to come, as well as instruction on a few new embroidery stitches. With those alarming threats, she finally made her exit.

"I insist you be flattered, Martha," I declared emphatically. "For look at what we endure for the pleasure of your company."

"Shhhh..." Cassie cautioned.

"It is bad enough to be a spinster, but must they also be pathetic and dull? Can they not exert themselves?" I continued.

"Where is your charity?" Cassie chided. "She does harm to no one."

"But she is an ugly foreshadowing that turns my heart cold. We may all come to be Miss Stents ourselves ... unequal to anything and unwelcome to everybody," I declared.

Martha reminded me that I had always said it was better to wind up alone than to be in a loveless marriage. I could not deny it. I had always clung to those lofty ideals. What I did not always take into account is that single women have a dreadful propensity for being poor.

Martha confessed, "I fear destitution as well. More than I have ever discussed. But it need not be your fate, Jane. If you truly desire security, I hear there is a candidate who would be happy to oblige ... and no, do not blame Cassandra, for it was Mrs. Lefroy who has kept me informed."

"Martha, you dispose of me without hesitation. When you know that a stupid man would be the end of me."

"Jane, I am coming to think that love is a luxury, and one that is outside our budget. In order to avoid a future of poverty, perhaps you should be willing to endure something less than ideal," Martha suggested.

"Do not make light of what must be endured. Reverend Blackall ... in his nightrobe ... ready to exercise his conjugal privileges!"

Cassie tried to silence me, but, in all truth, if I could not broach the subject in this company, how was I ever to work it out? For if marriage consisted only of a series of platonic meetings over teas and suppers, I supposed I could reconcile myself to just about any partner. But the physical intimacies … did they not demand that a husband be handsome and worthy of respect, as a bare minimum requirement for marital happiness? If a woman settled for less, would she not approach every nightly encounter with dread?

"If the time comes, we shall find ourselves capable of enduring what millions of our sex have suffered, and with little complaint," Martha advised.

I objected. "Suffer? Why should we suffer? The ladies who became acquainted with *Tom Jones* did not seem to be suffering…Yes, yes, I know it is a fiction, but torn from real life, surely. If it were not … enjoyable … why so much adultery?"

Neither Cassie nor Martha could formulate an answer. Our discussion certainly would have benefitted from the inclusion of a lady with more expertise than ourselves. But I was able to turn their ignorance and squeamishness to my advantage. There was no more talk of Reverend Blackall that night.

The next day, I was pleased to take Papa under my wing and show him the prettiest areas of the promenade and beach. And I must confess, I was also escaping the laundry and baking duties that Cassie and Mama had plunged into with such enthusiasm. It was quite right that the Austen family show their gratitude to Mr. Shaw by taking over all of the household drudgeries, and I heartily approved. Even though I could not heartily join in. What a useless creature I was. It was well I was not burdened with more conscience in those matters.

Papa walked slowly, but appreciatively along the beach. The cares of teaching and farming and sermon-making were fading into distant memory, and though some might have felt adrift at such a major change of life, he embraced it as he ought ... precious moments of freedom for a lifetime of good service. He was refreshed by the sea air and lulled into thoughtful reflection by the pounding of the waves.

"Jane, it appears that Reverend Blackall is very much interested in making you an offer, and if I know you at all, I should say he is about to be disappointed."

"You know me very well," I confirmed.

"I can guess at some of your objections. He is overly eager to impress you with his prospects. I was a courting man myself once upon a time, and so I can forgive him for that. But in his favour, he does have some very good connections, not the least of which is your dear friend Mrs. Lefroy. But more than that, he offers to provide you where I have failed: a secure and comfortable future."

I had not previously realized how much guilt Papa shouldered for want of being able to bestow Cassie and me with dowries or consequence that would have guaranteed our eligibility. He had tended carefully to the education of our brothers, exploited every relation and acquaintance to see them safely launched into university, the Royal Navy, and the clergy. But his financial struggles had impeded his ability to amass any real material legacy. I could not allow him to reproach himself thus.

"Cassie and I are full of gratitude and very contented. And proud, so terribly proud, of the kindest, the most intelligent, and most hard-working paragon of fatherhood that has ever walked the earth," I declared.

He was soothed, but his mind was still on practicalities.

"This paragon will not be around forever," he worried.

"Then let us not forget Edward. For he will never forget us, and there are a multitude of properties on his estate. I have not the smallest doubt that he will secure a roof over our heads, if it comes to that. So no more worries. Or regrets. Not on such a fine day."

With that comfort, we were both at peace, and by and by, I convinced him to shed his shoes and acquaint himself with the sea's robust charm.

A fortnight into our visit, I had acquired such a degree of comfort with Sidmouth that I did not hesitate to venture forth alone. On this occasion, I had been entrusted to obtain some medication to soothe Mama's mosquito bites. I myself had not been troubled by them. Was it my diet or my disposition that made my blood so unappetizing? How unfortunate that I was no longer writing outlandish tales to entertain a schoolroom of young boys, for an irritable old woman being driven to madness by a relentless assault of demon mosquitoes would have been a very pretty plot. With my thoughts thus employed, I came upon Lieutenant Frederick Barnes climbing out of a carriage before I had a chance to evade the encounter. He had a manservant with him, who unloaded a small, very modest case of luggage onto the road.

"I am very sorry, sir, to inconvenience Mrs. Doherty and yourself in this manner," the servant apologized.

"Nonsense, man. Take all the time that is required. Drop us a note in a week's time and let us know how she is doing. And take this," the lieutenant commanded.

He shoved a jingly bag of coins into his servant's hand,

waving off protests.

"Secure the carriage, Norton. Your coach will be here shortly. Miss Austen. What a ... pleasant surprise."

With that, he bid farewell to Norton and fell in step with me as I continued my journey.

"If I may inquire ..." I began curiously.

"Ah, his mother is in London, and in very poor condition. So we have given him leave to attend to her needs until she recovers. Or until she doesn't recover."

"And you pay him, though he will not be providing you with any services?" I asked astounded.

"The expenses of life are unending, and he is a very deserving man. However, should you ever have a chance to meet my Aunt Doherty, I should appreciate your not mentioning the coin. She would not see the logic of it," he chuckled lightly.

Hmmm. This was most unexpected, and undeniably kind. Particularly in light of some of his previous offenses. The character of a man is not so simple a thing to work out. Had his odious nature largely been a product of my own invention? Would it really be so terrible if Cassie had actually attached herself to this man? I was at a loss for answers to these questions, a state of indecisiveness that was much more uncomfortable than the certainty of loathing. When the lieutenant bid me farewell at the pharmacist's door, I resolved to confront Cassie and put these confusions to rest, one way or the other.

It was not until bedtime that a stretch of privacy was at hand.

"Cassie, I chanced to meet Lieutenant Barnes on the

promenade this afternoon," I began.

"Oh, no, Jane. Please tell me you were able to exhibit a modicum of good manners."

"As you well know, I have never had a high regard for the gentleman. He has irritated me at every turn. But after this afternoon, I am led to conclude that he is … not entirely worthless," I conceded.

"Such praise would make him blush."

"I am in earnest, Cassie. Perhaps he is not the man I would have chosen for you. No, he certainly is not. But if you have feelings for him, I shall accustom myself to the idea and treat him with due courtesy. And wish you every happiness."

"Jane, what are you thinking!? The lieutenant and I have no such understanding."

She laughed at me so heartily, that I was quickly convinced of my error. Well, this was welcome news. The no longer quite so odious lieutenant was still not someone I wanted to welcome into the Austen family, and this was a most desirable turn of events. Though I should never have been subjected to such disturbing conjectures to begin with.

"Cassie, you should not have misled me so. If I had known there was nothing between you, I should not have wasted so much effort being civil to him," I complained.

"Effort, you call it? He would need a microscope to uncover that small amount of effort. But have no fear, Jane. It is much more likely that your *efforts* went entirely without notice, and you will never be troubled by his gratitude or any other such repercussions," Cassie continued.

Now that I had arrived at a more serene perception, Cassie thought it safe to mention that Lieutenant Barnes had extended an open invitation to us to make use of his family's library. From the sound of it, it rivaled our old Steventon collection in size, and dwarfed kind Mr. Shaw's meager offerings. Yesterday, I should have been reluctant to deepen Cassie's acquaintance with the lieutenant. Now that that danger has been averted, the lure of a fresh supply of reading was more than I could resist. I gave Cassie leave to accept the invitation, and thought to make a few changes to my character sketches before I retired.

> *Mr. Darcy shrugged his shoulders as his former servant removed the offending dog for execution.*
> *"I am in a charitable frame of mind. I shall withhold a full week of your salary, in lieu of dismissal."*
> *"Yes sir, thank you sir," the man sighed gratefully.*
> *"... and spare the dog," Darcy conceded.*

With that revision, my own generosity was exhausted, and I had no difficulty in falling into a deep and peaceful sleep.

CHAPTER SEVEN
A SURPRISING TWIST OF FATE

I would not call Mrs. Doherty's summer home a great estate, but it was certainly one of the largest houses in Sidmouth, and its library did not disappoint. But before its riches could be uncovered, there was the small matter of paying court to Mrs. Doherty. She was just above fifty years of age, and expensively attired. The corners of her mouth slanted downwards in a more or less permanent scowl. Perhaps a smile would reverse that effect, but none made an appearance during our visit. Mrs. Doherty was very much of an old family upbringing and it was apparent that she was rather uneasy that her nephew had extended such a familiar invitation to the two unmarried daughters of a country parson. When she inquired as to how he had made our acquaintance, Lieutenant Barnes recounted for her the foot injury in Kent that had required his assistance.

"In my day, a well-brought up young woman never became acquainted with young gentlemen without a proper introduction," the dowager pronounced sternly.

"There I must place blame on your nephew," I

defended. "For I begged him to leave me in the ditch and go fetch someone who could make the introduction."

Mrs. Doherty was not amused, and still troubled by romantic scenarios. How comforted she would be if she knew how little cause there was for worry. Still, there was nothing we could do to directly allay her suspicions, and I knew that the lieutenant would eventually calm her fears after our departure. The lieutenant caught my eye and tipped his head in a note of apology. At least he had a few good-mannered impulses. Soon enough, he announced that he must honour his promise to show us the library, and his aunt was reluctantly forced to give up her vigil.

I had been promised almost two thousand volumes, and it seemed to me that number was happily exceeded. Why had we not discovered this treasure earlier in our holiday? Oh, yes, because our host had been so unbearably disagreeable. But on this day, for the sake of borrowing privileges, I was highly motivated to feign perfect cordiality. Cassie quickly settled in a comfortable armchair with a volume of sonnets, and it fell on me to be the object of Lieutenant Barnes' hospitality. The size of the collection *was* daunting, and so I actually did not mind an orientation. Though I immediately had to scold him for placing the works of the brilliant Crabbe in the same case as the dreadful Addison.

"I confess the library has been arranged by alphabet rather than by merit. Where would you suggest the Addison go?"

"Do you not have a rickety chair in need of propping up?"

Far from insulted, he actually seemed pleased to host a reader with such firm opinions. He offered a few of his own, and I confess, with contrary motives, I did pull a few of his favorites off the shelf, to confirm, if I could, the wrongheadedness of his approval. But books were not the only objects of interest. The room was filled with several large tables, some covered with maps, and one held drawings and graphs detailing the build of a large military craft.

"There is something odd about the hull of this ship. Is this a working vessel?" I inquired.

"No. Not at present. It is my own design. I have been on ships for so long that I cannot help but speculate on what may improve them … to withstand an assault better. Or the storms that now overturn them."

"Are you a shipbuilder?" I wondered.

"I am not, Miss Jane."

"Architect? Engineer?"

"Neither. Though such a life would have suited me well."

"And what is this contrivance?" I demanded. "If it does not violate military secrets."

"*That* is a device for pulling the salt out of seawater. For lack of fresh water is always an impediment. Techniques exist, but they must be improved to process a higher volume. Not only for wartime, but civilian voyages as well."

Here was an intriguing twist … more usefulness in him than I had been willing to see. "Have you had these designs assessed, Lieutenant? They could turn the tide!"

"You flatter me," he smiled.

"That was not my intention," I admonished.

Of course, there was probably some tragic flaw in his designs. But I could only applaud the effort. Even away from battle, it was clear that his thoughts were still on the war effort, which was undeniably commendable, though it pained me to acknowledge it. I moved to a small collection of books nearby and pulled one out.

"I am afraid those manuals will be of little interest to you," the lieutenant cautioned.

"Maritime Regulations by Hobson. I well recall being drilled on chain of command in the event of heavy senior losses," I informed him. "But you do not have the latest edition."

"I have underestimated you."

"There you are in large company. You have perhaps forgotten my two brothers in the Navy. Frank was recently given command of his own frigate. Charles is on a sloop, guarding trade routes," I boasted.

"I am sure they serve with great distinction," the lieutenant offered.

"Yes, but ... it is hard. We are ever waiting on assurances in the post."

The lieutenant nodded, quite familiar with the anxiety of families, starving for news. I continued my progress around the room, stopping at another memorable volume.

"Sir Charles Grandison! Now there is an old friend," I exclaimed.

"Is not marriage the highest state of friendship that mortals can know?" the lieutenant quoted.

"That is my favorite line. You have read it on more than one occasion yourself."

"I confess I have. It is a fairy tale, of course."

"Of course," I agreed.

I would not have him see me as some starry-eyed romantic. What a mortifying thought. Particularly as he had recently been unveiled as a man of some logic and scientific inclination. Not to mention, it was quite important that he unreservedly report to his aunt that the Austen girls had invaded their social sphere for literature, not love.

I was able to collect eight books from their library, a satisfying bounty. But even when distributed between Cassie and myself, it would have been a burdensome walk home. I did not protest when Cassie accepted a carriage ride home, for borrowing the books had already indebted us. Why struggle over an additional favour?

I carried away enough books to be generous with Martha, whom I spent the greater part of the following afternoon with at a picnic on the beach, just fifty yards short of the waves. Martha was heartily grateful to share in our library plunders. I suspected that she would welcome any rescue from the tedium of long evenings of Miss Stent's helpful instruction. Indeed, Martha could also read the stories to her tiresome hostess, as such activity was almost certain to induce sleep in a non-inquisitive mind.

"Now, you owe me some entertainment," I demanded. "What news of Steventon? How do our old friends get on? The Biggs? Any beaus? Any engagements?"

"You should know better, Jane. Nothing changes. The Biggs sisters, dear girls, are as unlikely to wed as I, even though their comfort is much more enviable. There is so little society to draw on, so few new faces. You and Cassie are the lucky ones. Godmersham and Sidmouth and Bath. When I read your letters, I could almost pretend that I led an exciting life, myself."

Dear Martha was a needed reminder of the relatively minor nature of my own complaints. She lived a Spartan existence with an ailing mother (truly ailing, unlike mine) and after her mother eventually dies, her prospects would become even bleaker. She was so beyond the age of marriage that I could not even hope for her. No inheritance to anticipate. No annuity. But that again reminded me of my own lack of independence. My father's pension would end with his death. And though my parents still dreamed their daughters would be spoiled for choice by the eligible men of Bath, I did not have the heart to share their delusions.

"Martha, do you ever look around at life, at your life, and think, how did I arrive at this moment? Do you remember being twelve? Or fifteen? And the absolute certainty of the happy future that was waiting ahead? And being so impatient for it. Never imagining that you would have the sort of life that you pitied and ridiculed. Never imagining that the happy future was a just a phantom."

"Jane, I should try to pull you out of such dark thoughts. But these last few days in Miss Stent's society have led to some somber reflections. Yes, why could a brighter future not have unfolded? Why did Mr. W. never ask me to marry him?"

Oh, I had hoped that the thought of that unsuccessful encounter, some ten years previous, had faded from Martha's memory. We had long ago dispensed with his name, in the hopes of lessening his shadow. He was to her life as Tom Lefroy had been to mine: the end of romantic faith.

"He was undeserving," I denounced.

"Mr. W. was undeserving," Martha agreed. "But why was there no Mr. X, Y, or Z to follow him? Does life really only present one opportunity and no more?"

We were silent and I was sure both our thoughts turned to Cassie and her dearly departed fiancé. In all my life, I had never known a kinder and worthier soul than my sister, so yes, if she was only offered one chance for happiness, then Martha and I could not hope for better.

"But now, it is my duty to preach contentment," Martha commanded. "We have books, we have sun, we have the sea, and we have each other, Jane. Promise we shall always have each other. For without your friendship, the future would be bleak indeed."

It was an opportune moment to introduce a scheme that had been floating in my head for some years now.

"Whenever you do lose your dear mother, Martha, you will ever be welcome in the Austen household."

"I shall always look forward to visiting the Austens. I hope I shall come to know Bath well."

"Not visiting, Martha. Coming to live with us. A real sister, as you always have been."

Martha was momentarily stunned. And then the tears began to flow. But happy tears, surely?

"Jane, I should like nothing better. But we cannot presume that your parents would welcome the addition."

I laid out my plan. Mama was already fond of Martha, and with just a little exertion, Martha could make herself even more agreeable. During her visits, she could offer cheerful assistance with chores. Humour Mama's medical complaints. Make herself indispensable. When Cassie was called away to play nursemaid to our expectant sister-in-laws, Martha would be there to fill the void. I should do my own part by becoming more and more useless, so that Martha's assistance would grow to be essential. We would have a few years to wage this campaign, but when the time came, there was every possibility that Mama herself would extend the invitation and take full credit for the idea. Martha did not require much convincing, for it echoed a dream she had not dared voice. It was an inventive scheme, but entirely plausible. The gloom of the day was lifted. No longer the victims of fate, Martha and I delighted at the thought of at last taking some command of our own lives.

However, before Martha could be added to the Austen family, someone else clearly needed to be removed. Reverend Blackall had recently taken every opportunity to insinuate himself amongst us. He was to join us at tonight's Italian opera. Sidmouth did not have the cultural advantages of Bath, but its population was large enough to support weekly concerts and recitals. A welcome diversion, but likely to be marred by Reverend Blackall's presence. Was it not enough that we were to see him at tomorrow morning's sermon? Which only provided a reprieve of some twelve hours. What a tedious courtship life had presented me with. I had previously thought evasion to be my best tactical maneuver.

Mr. Collins and Mrs. Bennett exited the barn, where they had hoped to find Elizabeth. Outside the barn, large ten foot piles of hay awaited bundling.

"I do not know where she has gotten to, Mr. Collins," Mrs. Bennett apologized. "For I know she is most anxious to receive you."

"I am the happiest of men, to hear such assurances, Mrs. Bennett. Though I do confess that my connections and securities are of such a nature that I am certain that any young lady of good sense would be

heartily grateful for my offer."

"Indeed, Mr. Collins, Lizzie will be overjoyed to hear your proposal; it will be the answer to all her prayers. Come. Perhaps she has returned to the house."

Not twenty seconds after their departure, one of the haystacks shook and erupted, and a disheveled Elizabeth emerged from her hiding place. She let out an audible sigh of relief, contented with her temporary reprieve.

But it had become clear that my own situation would require something more definitive. I had once cringed at the prospect of a proposal from the Reverend, but now I longed for the chance to present him with a loud resounding refusal. It would be the only way to put an end to him.

The opera was our first opportunity to see the Assembly Hall. It was a newly constructed building, satisfyingly grand and ornate, and a fitting home for the best of Sidmouth's concerts and balls. Unfortunately, it inspired the Reverend's inclinations to perform; he paraded his expertise in operas, providing interpretations between every song. The singer's voice was beautiful even without translation, and admittedly, the details of the story certainly enhanced her performance. Still, I was restless, and one hour of entertainment was all I could bear. I excused myself, and doubtless, the Reverend assumed that I would return shortly.

But I had no such intention. I meant to head out into the night air, but I was diverted into an exploration down a tempting hallway of this grand public ballroom. What lay behind these doors? I spied candlelight coming through the cracks of one not quite closed. My shameless excursion was rewarded; it was a practice room with a pianoforte inside, a rather nice one at that. I darted in, and hearing some steps in the nearby reception room, quickly closed the door behind me. Here was a great means to keep myself occupied. I hoped the concert would go on for another full hour, as there are few things I enjoyed so much as playing music.

I was engrossed in my playing and did not hear the door open behind me. But I certainly heard it close, and I whirled around to see an apologetic Lieutenant Barnes.

"I hoped there was better entertainment to be found in these back rooms. And so I was right. A very pretty tune, Miss Jane," he praised.

"I do not play for the enjoyment of others. Only myself," I replied, coolly.

"That is most ungenerous. Why should you not share your talents with the world?" the lieutenant scolded.

"First of all, the ladies who share their talents with the world do so with one object, and that is to attract a marriage proposal. Hardly a charitable motive. After that object is secured, she is free to abandon the pastime," I explained.

The lieutenant was full of objections. He had known many gifted young ladies who evidenced a true love of music for its own worth, including his younger sister who had a wondrous gift with the pianoforte. And *she* was married. I wondered how many times he had seen her since she married.

"There have been three visits," he recalled.

"And did she play? This prodigy? Or did she step aside for the unmarried ladies?"

The lieutenant stared at me in mute revelation, followed by an amused chuckle.

"And secondly? You have another objection to sharing your talent?"

"Only this: my playing does not qualify as talent. No, do not indulge me in false compliments. My playing is of a mediocre quality and can bring pleasure only to myself. Society must prevail without the contribution of my talents, for I have none."

"What? None? Surely you can sing?"

"Surely not."

"Harp? Drawing? Needlework? Are you in earnest? Are you absolutely free of talent? That is most refreshing."

What a strange idea. "You find this a cause for celebration?" I asked.

"Indeed, for you know not how exhausting it is for gentlemen to continually be expected to appreciate a woman's talents. Hours of recitals. Endless displays of embroidery. A woman without talent is a rare find."

He gave all appearance of sincerity, but I had never heard an odder sentiment.

"To look at you," I mused, "One would never suspect such a peculiarity of mind."

He slid down onto the bench beside me.

"You have the appearance of normalcy yourself," he returned.

Before I had the chance to rebuke him, he began to play a tune with his free hand. It was a simple Scottish jig, quite familiar to any student of the instrument.

"Can you lend me your left hand, Miss Jane?"

I could not resist the novelty of the experiment. I joined in, matching his tempo, which was rather sprightly. Owing to his cast, he could not bend his left arm, and the fingers of that hand tapped soundlessly on his lap, as my right hand did on mine. It was a most unusual duet, but though unrehearsed, we managed to stay together, and were both pleased with the result.

"You play well … for a man," I conceded. For as a rule, gentlemen did not seem to exert much effort in providing musical entertainment for others.

"I have learned today that fine playing is a matrimonial inducement for a partner of quality. Had I known earlier, I should have applied myself even more."

"For accomplished *women*, Lieutenant. I did not say it worked in the other direction. But you do play well enough for your own enjoyment. And for mine."

"That resembled a compliment!" He cocked his head in surprised amusement. "I rather expected a scathing critique."

I was obliged to acknowledge that few could withstand the barrage of bad manners I had thrown in his path. And he had passed all tests.

"That would be to little purpose, for you never take offense … despite my best efforts."

This confession made us both smile.

"You take great enjoyment in laughing at your fellow man," he observed.

"I will not deny it. But I hope I never ridicule what is wise or good."

"And do you laugh at yourself?"

"When I am not busy laughing at others."

"And when is that?" he inquired skeptically.

I thought for a moment. "Tuesdays."

"Oh, blessed day! I shall mark my calendar."

I could not repress another smile, and my last wall of resistance was overcome. He was actually revealing himself to be a rather amiable type, with none of the blandness typically associated with the phrase. And he clearly found my company agreeable, though I had done little to earn his good opinion. Now, his eyes latched onto mine and I saw naught but good humour and approval.

"I have been informed that your family will be extending their stay in Sidmouth," he observed.

"Yes, at least another fortnight until our new home in Bath has completed repairs."

"Then you will be here for next week's dance at this same Assembly Hall. Do you enjoy dancing, Miss Jane?"

Was this an idle inquiry? Or prelude to an invitation? "Yes, I suppose I do."

"Then may I reserve the honour of the first two dances? My cast comes off in three days, and by the ball, I am sure I will be a fit partner."

"I shall be the judge of that, Lieutenant," I said with mock sternness, which did no harm. For in the blink of an eye, we had become friends. "But if you are out of practice, you may even out your roughness with me, after which, the fine ladies of Sidmouth can reap the benefits."

"I have already secured the only dance partner of any interest to me in Sidmouth. You are singular, Miss Jane. And you have ruined me for other company."

There was no mistaking him. His words and his tone were full of deep admiration. I needed to remain calm, but my pounding heart was undermining me. I made my way towards the door.

"You know I care not for flattery, Lieutenant," I blushed.

"Then I shall endeavor to restrain myself, Miss Jane."

I hurriedly made my exit as soon as I saw his broad smile, as I did not want him to catch sight of mine.

CHAPTER EIGHT
THE RETURN OF HOPE

The most welcome event in the Austen household was the arrival of a letter, and this morning, we were treated to two of them: one from Charles, an incomparably comforting assurance of his safety, and another from our old friend Mrs. Anne Lefroy. The latter was addressed to Mama, but I knew that I should soon have it memorized by heart. I tore open Charles' letter first and the family and Mr. Shaw gave me their full attention.

Charles recounted one recent victorious battle, but I am sure he under-reported it to avoid causing alarm. He did provide the number of casualties and losses, which seemed considerable for the winning side. However, he was in good health, and thanked us for all our recent correspondence ... sent some three months ago! He also spoke of illnesses and floggings, promotions and scheming plots.

"It is unfortunate," I mused, "That Charles or Frank could not break their arm and be sent home for a two month leave for recovery."

"Jane, you could not wish such a thing on our dear

brothers," Cassie reprimanded.

"It is a small thing compared to the daily uncertainties of battle. Would not you love to have Charles here safe with us for two months? Or better still … a broken leg and four months of leave. Can you not see that a little physical discomfort on his part will be the sacrifice for the peace of mind and enjoyment of his company that will benefit his entire family?"

"You are heartless and selfish, Jane," Mama responded; I knew that we were in full agreement.

"Hmmph! And what says our dear Mrs. Lefroy?" I asked.

Mama opened up her letter and read it first in full silence. Whatever she read appeared to cause her some agitation.

"No bad news, I hope," Papa inquired.

"No, indeed. She is in health, and very happy to announce the engagement of her nephew Tom Lefroy to a Miss Paul. Her father owns quite a lot of property in Essex and she brings thirty thousand pounds to the union."

The eyes of all my family turned upon me. Mr. Shaw was unconcerned and serene, as often happened when a shared family understanding took a confusing turn for him.

"Well, he had to marry someone, did he not?" I offered, trying to ease the general discomfort. "After all … after all … he is the sort of young man who would have no trouble securing a bride, once he has made up his mind that he is ready for a match. Indeed, I have noticed that any man can marry, if he but wants it. There is no question that a man who wants to marry does not end up married. Even Reverend Blackall will marry, depend on it. Within two years at most."

"Jane," Cassie commiserated.

"Well, I shall have to write to Mrs. Lefroy and offer my congratulations. For I think things have unfolded as they should have. Truly. Since his unhappiness would do me no material good, then I am free to wish him every happiness. Truly, Cassie."

And until I uttered the words, I did not know that I could mean them. But my heart had mended over, the scar inconsequential. And it was almost alarming to know how much of this healing was of very recent occurrence. My mind turned again to Lieutenant Frederick Barnes, as it had some dozen times since we last parted. I almost laughed aloud to think how much I had once disliked him, though for all the tea in China, I could not at this moment, remember why. His partiality brought another flooding to my cheeks. How odd that he should prefer me to any other. And what a handsome man he was. I had noticed it before, but did my best to take no notice. What should I wear to the dance? Despite my command that he refrain from more compliments, I was of course, determined to choose a gown that would challenge his resolve. These exquisitely unsettling thoughts threatened to turn into a tidal wave. To secure a reprieve, I challenged Mr. Shaw to a game of chess.

The following day brought another long walk on the beach with Cassie and Martha. A large Naval ship on the horizon brought matters of war to the forefront. We obliged Martha on the minute details of Charles' letter. Having held him in her arms when he was a baby, she now took a most gratifying interest in his well-being.

"Flogging! Are we assured that Charles and Frank have

never been subjected?" Martha worried.

"Definitely not," Cassie asserted. "They have never mentioned such a thing."

"Nor would they," I mused. "Even if true. For fear of worrying us. But it is most unlikely. They are intelligent and loyal and would never do anything to earn such a barbaric punishment."

"I know it is harsh, but is not the military founded on discipline and does it not have to be maintained at all costs?" Cassie ventured.

I objected, "Discipline, yes. But why should our sailors be treated worse than our prisoners? How are they to fulfill their duties when they are beaten in body and spirit? How does this strengthen our forces? Some have even died in the process."

"Surely there are better methods to ensure obedience," Martha wondered.

"I am sure a day without food would work well for most of them," I suggested. "Perhaps two days if they have done something particularly heinous. But at least then, their health and strength could be restored with a single meal."

"When Frank and Charles reach the highest ranks, you may advise them accordingly, and if they are receptive, then Jane Austen will have made her mark on the British Navy," Cassie mocked. "Oh dear, Jane, do not become agitated. Lieutenant Barnes approaches with his brother. But I will occupy him and you will not have to trouble yourself conversing with him."

"Cassie, that will not be necessary."

Cassie was puzzled, but the men were upon us before I could offer explanation.

"Lieutenant Barnes. Dr. Barnes. What a pleasant

coincidence," Cassie greeted them.

Whether or not it could be termed a coincidence, I had my suspicions.

"And your arm is healed," Cassie continued.

So it was. The lieutenant's cast had been removed. He bent his arm stiffly at the elbow.

"Yes, I am nearly restored," the lieutenant replied.

Martha was introduced to the gentlemen and we all proceeded together. But it was not long before the lieutenant and I found seclusion several yards beyond our companions.

"And did my brother and I intrude on any particular topic?" the lieutenant inquired.

"Flogging," I announced, happy to shock him. "We just received a letter from one of our naval brothers, Charles."

"He does not spare you," the lieutenant observed.

"We have always begged him to be open," I assured him.

"So then, what are your thoughts on flogging, Miss Jane?"

"I think that inflicting injury and bloodshed on English sailors is best left in the hands of the enemy."

He gazed at me with such a curious expression. "Yes, indeed. Our adversary needs no further assistance."

"How long have you been in service, Lieutenant?"

"Only six years ... though it has the feel of ten," he reflected.

I drew him out, for I wanted to hear his whole story. He had not chosen the Navy for career as had my brothers who joined up when they were fourteen and twelve years of age. The lieutenant joined after the war began, determined to be of some service. I inquired as to his profession, before the war.

"Well, I was graduated from Cambridge two years earlier …" he began.

"We are an *Oxford* family, Lieutenant…But, continue," I commanded.

We both smiled at the rivalry.

"I had long intended to enter the clergy. It seemed a practical path, as I did not find the law compelling, and did not share my brother's love of cadavers. I was most fortunate to find a parish soon after."

"Did you enjoy your work?" I asked.

"It suited well enough. But then the war began. And I could no longer bear my idleness. Bonaparte roused me to duty."

"He abuses the virtue of ambition. Why does he need the Pyramids?"

"Or Italy, Switzerland, Austria, for that matter. Clearly he has an eye for beauty. His ambitions rise as ours cool."

"He will never invade England," I asserted.

"He would take that as challenge," the lieutenant countered. "We lose allies at every turn. And we cannot fight this war alone. There is peace ahead, Miss Jane. A bitter peace that will not be lasting. But it will provide the briefest respite."

"Needed by all," I concurred. "Will you remain in the Navy?"

He hesitated, as if broaching a difficult subject.

"There are many things to take into consideration. One is my fitness for service. This is not my first injury. I have had bullet wounds to my left shoulder and right leg. And had one troublesome concussion."

I winced at his ordeals, but I could not let him see that I cared.

"You are clumsy, Lieutenant."

He smiled as warmly as if I had reached out and touched his hand.

"My shoulder recovered, but not as well as it ought. My rifle aim was somewhat compromised. And my brother fears with another trauma on the same side, that there may be no further improvements. He discourages a return to service."

"He seems a very good doctor," I ventured.

"I believe so. Though not unbiased."

"And what says the Navy?" I wondered anxiously.

"My captain values my navigation talents, but I fear, is little impressed by my battle skills. At any rate, he does advocate my return to civilian life."

I struggled to steady my voice. "And what is it that *you* want, Lieutenant?"

"In truth, I should very much like to pursue my designs and see if they have any merit. I should like to fulfill my obligations to … my family. And I should like to be happy, Miss Jane … if it is not too much to ask."

His gaze was too direct and too unsettling. I looked towards the others, who were headed in our direction.

"Was it a coincidence? Your coming across us out here?"

"It was not, Miss Jane."

Hmmm. As I suspected. We were reunited with the others, and Cassie surveyed me quickly to see how I had fared, and was surprised to find me so peacefully disposed.

"Jane, Dr. Barnes has been telling us that he provides daily assistance in a convalescence home for wounded sailors," Cassie informed.

"I have to occupy my time more productively than defeating Frederick at chess," the doctor teased.

"Now, I will not allow you to make the ladies understand I am always on the losing side," the lieutenant objected, with mock offense.

"Nothing of the sort," Cassie soothed. "But he did say there was a need for people to help read to the patients, and I thought Jane and I might be able to be of use."

"Certainly. We would love to," I responded quickly.

Oh, dear. That was too much enthusiasm.

"That is most kind. Of course, I expect you to return to our library and pilfer it to your heart's content," the lieutenant offered.

"Jane, that reminds me. I have two of the lieutenant's books to return to you, so that you may restore them," Martha remembered.

"Ah," the lieutenant noted. "You have founded a small regional branch of the Barnes family library, Miss Jane."

"Martha, you have given me away," I scolded.

But I knew the lieutenant did not mind. He was determined to be pleased with me. And I did not mind. For I was determined to test the limits of his indulgence. The gentlemen escorted us back to the promenade and we all parted with the certainty of an imminent reunion. Cassie was at last able to satisfy her curiosity.

"You are much changed towards the lieutenant, Jane."

"I have promised him the first two dances at the upcoming Assembly Ball," I announced breezily.

"Surely this is not the same man you spoke of in your letter? The insufferable lieutenant?" Martha marveled.

"The very same," I confirmed, somewhat sheepishly.

"How is it that you like him?" Cassie wondered.

"Well, he is not so very bad, is he?" I offered.

"And do you think that he likes you?" Martha asked

incredulously.

"Is that so difficult to believe?" I huffed.

"Not at all. I know you are capable of being quite charming and reasonable. I am sure he has seen your best side."

"No," I reflected. "He has seen my true side … and he likes me still."

Cassie and Martha were both struck dumb at this turn of events. Martha nudged me in the side.

"A naval man!" she enthused.

"Stop," I protested, but it was fairly unconvincing. I felt an old familiar giddiness start to take hold. It was somewhat altered by time and maturity. But love was threatening to storm the castle. And though I could and should, lessen the importance of it to others, I could not lie to myself and deny that my hopeful visions of happiness had risen from the ashes.

Our eventual appointment at the convalescent home turned into as much an education as it was a service. I prepared as best I could, more than aware that the stories that pleased me might not be of same interest to this tough weary audience. I knew not if they would warm to tales of battle and peril at sea, or if indeed, they required an escape from the troubling reminders of war and injury. Thus I brought a selection, including gothic horror, military heroism, and love triumphant. I should let them choose for themselves.

It was a quiet place, with some thirty beds filled, and divided amongst three large rooms. A majority of the residents were missing a limb. There were some moans of pain, and bustle of the attending staff. But most of the men stared wordlessly at the ceiling, or listlessly about them.

Cassie and I did garner quite a bit of interest upon our entry. We informed a nurse that we had been sent by Dr. Barnes, and she directed us to where we could be of greatest use. She was good enough to introduce us to our somber audience. I was seated in a chair, ideally situated between two cots, so that two might benefit from the reading. And if I took care to speak in a loud clear voice, the enjoyment might spread even beyond, to some three or four other neighboring occupants. I had meant to supply them with choice, but the sad and tentative atmosphere demanded the cure of a lively and diverting entertainment.

"Can I interest you gentlemen in a ghost story?" I inquired.

They nodded assent, and seemed greatly relieved. Perhaps they had been afraid that I was going to read Bible passages. But I am sure they were supplied with a weekly chaplain and did not require redundant messages of inspiration. And if not, then we should send Papa over, for his sermons had been widely praised.

I chose a magazine tale that I knew could be fitted in the space of two hours. If it proved to be too tiring for them, I could always return to continue. But at the midway mark, they were as engrossed as the schoolboys I had once held captive audience, and I carried on. After the grisly conclusion, there were a few smiles, some polite murmurs of appreciation, and a few silent heads tipped in gratitude. How little I had given, and how gratefully received. I knew I should come again.

"That'll keep a few up at night," one rough looking sailor remarked.

Whereupon began a most memorable encounter. He was certain that his grandfather's home had been haunted by a most disagreeable ghost, and he was much disappointed that I had no direct experience of them. When I asked what home he would return to after leaving this facility, he swore adamantly that he would not go back to prison, and that he had been promised he would not have to do so. So here was one of Charles' disreputable characters in the flesh. Or perhaps he had reformed and become a true and loyal servant to King and country. In any case, he had lost his leg and earned his pardon. I was most curious as to the nature of his crime, but having used the ghost story to lure him away from his troubles, it seemed unfair to turn his mind back to them. We chatted another fifteen minutes on inconsequential matters.

When we departed, Dr. Barnes was also making his exit. He thanked us for coming and we assured him that it had been mutually beneficial.

"Will you be returning soon to Portsmouth, Dr. Barnes?" Cassie asked.

"I promised that I would deliver Aunt Doherty back to her estate. And then I shall journey to my parents and enjoy a brief visit before I return to my practice."

"And where are your parents?" Cassie pried.

"Our family home is in Kent, where you first encountered my brother. He spent a month of recovery with family. But then Aunt Doherty imposed heavily and asked him to escort her to her summer house."

"He is your elder?" Cassie inquired.

"By two years."

"And he never married?"

I could have kicked her. How mortifying that Dr.

Barnes should suspect that these questions were on my behalf.

"Well, he certainly wanted to, as we all do, I suppose. But we cannot always control the circumstances of life."

"So, he was never engaged?" Cassie persisted.

"Indeed he was, though it was ended over six years ago. In truth, there was still a melancholy hanging over his head when he entered the Navy. I did suspect that he might never have joined had he not had that disappointment."

"Oh, dear," Cassie sympathized. "Is he fully reconciled?"

"Battle puts all things in perspective," Dr. Barnes assured us. "That episode is a bygone thing. And though he is naturally sobered by his naval duties, I believe he is otherwise in the best of spirits."

"He is of most admirable character," Cassie added.

"We take a great deal of pride in Frederick. He is the best of brothers. And sons."

"I would imagine he will also excel as a father. Does he take an interest in children?"

Cassie gave me a sideways glance. She really did deserve a thrashing. The doctor escorted us until our paths diverged and we assured him that we could make our own way home. As soon as he was beyond sight, I slapped Cassie across the backside and gave her arm a twisting pinch.

"Jane! Why are you not thanking me? You required information and I obtained it," she declared. It was quite a reversal for us, for I was always doing the teasing. But this was too large a matter. I felt excessively exposed, even to Cassie to whom I had always revealed everything. I did not want her expectations to wander too far, even though my own unruly heart and mind were losing all restraint. I wanted to become more intimately acquainted with Lieutenant Frederick Barnes. I wanted him to want the same. I wanted us to love each other. There. I could deny it no longer.

CHAPTER NINE
TOO GOOD TO BE TRUE

The next Sunday at church, I surreptitiously observed the Barnes family in the front pew. I confess I had seldom given the sermon so little attention. Indeed, if it had been one of my father's own sermons (which I had enjoyed immensely) I would not have been able to subdue my restless mind. Lieutenant Barnes knew that we were behind him. He had turned around when we entered. I was certain that we would congregate afterwards.

Perhaps my parents might even think to invite them over for tea again. I should have Cassie press that agenda. But Mrs. Doherty seemed unlikely to join them. Mr. Shaw's cottage was far too humble for her. I would have to find a way to ingratiate myself with that good lady. Cassie could have accomplished the mission with much greater ease, but I could certainly orchestrate sufficient charm and decorum that she might forget my earlier carelessness. Indeed, a woman of her years can be depended upon to be forgetful. We should never be great friends, but a peaceful treaty was a worthy goal.

As for his other relation, I liked Dr. Barnes immensely. A true gentleman, lacking all airs. I should very much like to introduce both men to my brothers one day. A shiver went up my spine. Would the future truly hold such encounters? And what of his younger sister, the piano prodigy? I knew naught else about her, but I was already prepared to be her devoted friend. Some forty-five minutes passed in this manner, and the sermon was finally done. Something about neighbours and charity and resisting temptations ... a bit meandering on the whole. But mercifully short. I suspected the pastor had to hasten to another church.

Outside, Cassie helpfully suggested to our parents that we linger in wait for the Barnes, as they had been so generous to us in the use of their library. My parents were happy to be reacquainted with both young men. Mrs. Doherty was introduced to them, and I could see that she was impatient to be on her way. I asked if she had enjoyed the sermon, and was happy to start her and Papa on the essay of what constituted a truly fine sermon. Frederick and I were able to back away from the others. I should say, the lieutenant and I, but inwardly, I was already addressing him on the most familiar of terms.

"And what did *you* think of the sermon, Miss Jane?"

"I confess, my mind was diverted to other pressing matters. Could you remind me of the particulars?"

He seemed ready to deliver a mock scolding, but then a moment of guilty hesitation, and a slightly bewildered look passed over his features.

"Lieutenant, you were in the front row. Surely, you can relate to me the contents of this sermon," I challenged.

"It was, uh ... something about ... neighbours ... and God."

We dared not laugh. I shook my head at our shameful inattention.

"May I inquire as to where your thoughts were directed, Miss Jane?"

"I was thinking ... of whether we could expect further tax increases on tea and sugar this quarter."

He smiled delightedly. "It is just as I thought. I suspected that our minds were similarly engaged."

What a glorious thing to know how mutual our preoccupation was. And how unfortunate that we were so soon to be parted. But even as I resented the war that would soon pull him away, I realized that I should never have had the opportunity to meet him without it. What had I done to deserve such good fortune? We did not have much time for further conversation when his brother informed us that their aunt was ready to be taken home.

"Andrew, you can see her home safely? Miss Austen and I were fully engrossed in the economic repercussions of recent embargoes. It is a matter that demands consummation."

"Then we shall see you at home, brother," Andrew replied agreeably.

A flurry of good-byes were bid, and the two groups parted our separate ways. It was apparent that all members of our respective families had been alerted to our partiality for one another. It was just as well; they must know at some time and best that they be mentally prepared. My family allowed the lieutenant and me to trail behind, with only an occasional glance backwards by both of my parents. They had had such high hopes for finding matches for their daughters in Bath. How surprised they must be to see the matter already settled. And no question but they would approve my choice: good standing in society, a good mind, and a temperament peculiar enough that we should fit like pieces of a puzzle.

When we arrived back at Mr. Shaw's cottage, the lieutenant did receive an invitation to tea, as I had anticipated. He accepted gladly and showed himself to have great ease in the company of those whom he was so barely acquainted. And though he was wearing his crisp uniform, he carried several logs of wood into the cottage, as Mr. Shaw's man had the day off, and the task would have been draining for either Papa or Mr. Shaw. What pride I already took in this man. Even as I exulted, some small dark corner of my mind warned ... had I not felt this happy certainty before, and did it not end in tears and crushing regret? This must be different. But how was it different? It was the difference between loving a dutiful boy and loving a man in control of his own destiny, perhaps. But something more ... if laid side by side, the virtues of the man won in every respect. I could even now be glad that I had lived through such disappointment, for it had left me unwed and available at exactly the right moment in time. I could only thank Providence. Thank my good fortune. Thank you for waiting for me Frederick. I know we shall be happy. The afternoon came to its lovely conclusion and we parted in anticipation of the Assembly Ball, just three days distant.

The following day was scheduled with lighthearted productivity. My gown intended for the dance wanted mending at the hem. Normally a wearying task, but I was cheered by the vision of the dancing soon to be at hand. I also wanted to refresh my memory on the nature of the dances and I troubled Cassie to practice with me in the parlour as best we could. I believe I got her to enjoy herself enough that she would certainly accompany me to the dance. We were thus employed, when we heard a carriage stop outside. Mr. Shaw was out of the house; who could it be? The mystery was soon answered, at least in part. It was Mrs. Doherty. As I had predicted, she was not at all pleased with Mr. Shaw's cottage, and requested that I accompany her for a walk. How unexpected. And yet I must make all efforts to make myself agreeable to the Lieutenant's family and here was a useful opportunity. We headed in the direction of the promenade, her carriage driver advancing slowly behind us.

"Miss Austen, my family and I will be receiving an old family friend very soon. Miss Alicia Whitley. She is a most accomplished and well-bred young lady, and of a most well-placed family."

"I shall be very pleased to make her acquaintance," I offered.

Mrs. Doherty smiled. It was a peculiar smile, and I had to say, not a kind one. "She is the young lady that Frederick is intended to marry."

She watched my features carefully, well aware of the shock she was inflicting.

"Intended? Intended to marry? I am certain that the lieutenant made no mention of an engagement, and I have heard him detail his upcoming plans at length," I countered.

"Nevertheless, they do have an understanding, and our family anticipates a wedding as soon as he leaves the Navy."

It was either truth or lie. Or willful misunderstanding. My thoughts did not know where to land.

"Miss … Miss …?" I stammered.

"Whitley," Mrs. Doherty supplied. "Miss Alicia Whitley."

"I cannot imagine that Lieutenant Barnes has had much

127

opportunity for courtship these past six years at sea."

"Their attachment is of longer duration. My nephew asked Miss Whitley to marry him before he left for the war."

So this *was* the same young lady that Dr. Barnes had mentioned when Cassie pressed him for information. But had he not assured us that Lieutenant Barnes' attachment for this lady had long ago faded? Either the brother or the aunt was mistaken. Only the lieutenant could break this stalemate. Happily, the thought of him brought me back to my original convictions. Did I not see the truth in his eyes, at our every encounter? Obviously, Mrs. Doherty would prefer him to make a different choice, but that was a disappointment she would be obliged to endure.

"Her family is most desirous of the match, and for my part, it is one of the only matches I should allow," Mrs. Doherty added.

"Allow!?" I tried to rein in my rising mood of indignation. "I have not known the lieutenant long, Mrs. Doherty, but well enough, I think, to know that he will follow his own convictions in this matter."

"No, you have not known him for long. Let me acquaint you with his circumstances. You see, after my son died two years ago, I chose Frederick to inherit all my estate. Everything. And it is quite a grand property. With over twenty servants. Doubtful you have ever seen such a place. But Frederick will carry the family tradition on with distinction."

"Of course," I managed, my mind swirling in confusion.

"But … it is not a fixed inheritance. It is a gift to him and all his heirs. In return, I ask him to honour the family and to join himself to the right wife. I know he will take this duty seriously, for if he does not, I should be forced to choose Andrew as heir, who I know would be most grateful and put the needs of the family first."

She finally had the reaction she wanted. I was stunned into a numb silence.

"But I do not think it will come to that," she continued. "For I have heard Frederick declare his feelings for Miss Whitley in the most ardent of terms. They are as well-matched as any couple could be. She will be here in time for the Assembly Ball. And then you will see for yourself."

She waved her cane at her carriage driver, and he quickly drew up, and made haste to help her inside.

"Good day, Miss Austen. I have enjoyed our talk."

I could barely move, certainly not in the direction of the cottage. I was unequal to any explanations, and had no energy for evasions or pretense. The promenade would be filled with unbearable society. I needed sparse population and such distance between myself and all others that none could see my anguish.

In short time, I was upon the waves. I slipped off my shoes to pace back and forth in the shallow waters, taking little notice as my dress became more and more soaked. I had opened up my heart again ... a heart almost fully mended by time. Like a careless guard leaving the gate open ... to plunder and destruction. Thus is wisdom learned, by those too foolish to heed the first lesson. What a wretched thing hope is. How relatively contented I was before it had re-entered my life and how unparalleled its ability to devastate. My prospects and future were exactly the same at this very moment as they had been two months ago ... or one year ago. It was a very logical assessment, but logic had no power to hold back the tears. They dropped like rain into the salty water below.

◇◇◇

The next day I was promised to a shopping expedition with Cassie and Martha. I had crawled into bed the previous evening, declining to satisfy Cassie's curiosity on the nature of Mrs. Doherty's visit. But with my dearest confidantes about me, I quickly dispatched the news. The sooner they had opportunity to comprehend, the sooner the matter could be buried in the past, and in time, to mercifully fall beyond memory. Cassie received the information with quiet gravity. She had witnessed so much to confirm the lieutenant's regard that she could not reconcile it with the reality of Miss Alicia Whitley. Martha was greatly concerned that I had been ill-used and had harsh words for the lieutenant.

"He must be the unworthiest of men to allow you to believe that matrimony was imminent. When all the while, he had an understanding with this lady? He is a scoundrel, and I wish him a life of misery," Martha declared.

"You will not say such things, Martha," I cautioned. "I cannot lay the blame at his feet, not even in part. I was never promised anything. We exchanged nothing but pleasantries and idle flattery. Truly. I was misled by my own imagination. But then, you are both quite familiar with my fanciful tales. It should not surprise you that I applied the same inventiveness to my own expectations. The gentleman cannot be faulted for any wild interpretations on my part. I can only promise you that the lesson has been well and truly understood, and for the very last time."

I did not wish to prolong the matter, and thankfully, interruption came in the form of a sixty year old man, with a walking cane, who greeted Cassie. She had made his acquaintance through Mr. Shaw. He walked arm-in-arm with a young lady who looked to be my age or younger, and who was introduced to us as Miss Jameson. He inquired after Mr. Shaw's health, was reassured, and was soon on his way.

"Father?" Martha inquired.

"Fiancé," Cassie explained.

"Oh dear," Martha flinched.

"It is not for us to judge," Cassie chided. "It is a match that suits their needs."

"Oh, it is an excellent match," I agreed. "He will certainly die before childbearing wears out her body. Her womb is most fortunate ... and her purse."

"That is a terrible view," Cassie objected.

"It is the fundamental essence of marriage ... a rational and soulless contract," I concluded. I felt newly fortified by facing these grim truths. And I wished to escape the discomfort of Cassie and Martha's concern. I invented a fictitious requirement for hair pins and arranged to meet them in half an hour's time at a tea shop.

It was only by chance that I happened to glance through the windows of a jewelry store to discover Lieutenant Frederick Barnes leaning over a display inside. Speak of the devil, indeed. It was a confrontation I had dreaded these last twenty-four hours, but I was instantly infused with more anger and less generosity than I had let on to my comrades. What had he to say for himself? I entered quietly and stood at his side.

"Shopping for a gift?" I asked.

I startled him, but he was pleasantly surprised to see me. His attentiveness was unchanged. But I knew that was about to come to an end.

"Miss Jane, indeed I am. For my mother. I was

contemplating this pendant."

It was a lovely thing, a handsome cameo bordered with pearls.

"She will be pleased, I assure you. But … nothing for Miss Whitley?" I inquired serenely.

Hmm. It was interesting sport, catching someone unawares in a falsehood or omission. He certainly seemed momentarily at a loss.

"What do you know of Miss Whitley?"

"Oh, nothing, I assure you. I know not if she is short or tall, silent or sociable, intelligent or deficient. But I am sure she will be expecting a gift. Or so your aunt led me to understand."

"My aunt!"

"Yes, your aunt. On whom your fortunes now depend. You are to inherit her estate. Is that correct?"

"Yes, I am to inherit."

"It is just as I thought," I accused.

"Inheritance is generally taken as a good thing. But your perverse nature takes a different view. Enlighten me."

"Those who accept family money must also accept family expectations. You will marry Miss Whitley and you will take over your aunt's estate."

"No. Whatever my aunt may have told you, I have no understanding with Miss Whitley. I did ask for her hand … some six years ago. And I was refused. And that was the end of it."

"Not the end, surely, for is Miss Whitley not to be a guest at your aunt's house at any moment?"

He sighed. "My aunt and Miss Whitley's parents may wish and scheme as much as they like. But I remain free to follow my own inclinations."

"Hmmph! Free to do as you are told," I countered. "I have no doubt your family will find you as obedient as your captain does."

"I am being tried for crimes I have not yet committed," he objected.

"But you will." I backed away towards the door, unwilling to relent. I had said enough. I had made it clear that I was impervious to any more deceptions or delusions. Let him deceive himself if he needed to. I exited to a much needed breeze of sea air.

My relief was but brief. The lieutenant was soon at my side.

"Firstly, I do apologize, Miss Jane, for the manner in which you have received this information. You would have heard about the estate soon enough, but I did make a decision to hold it back. Perhaps my pride will not reflect well on me, but I did not wish to be ... regarded ... for my fortune. But for myself alone. Can you forgive me for my silence on that matter?"

Perhaps I could credit him with worthy intentions in not making a show of his impending wealth. Indeed, after having listened to Reverend Blackall relentlessly detail his own happy circumstances, the lieutenant's reserve came close to being commendable. Still, that was a small matter laid beside the larger issue of Miss Whitley. He detected where my thoughts had turned.

"I did love Miss Whitley once. But no more. Her family wanted her to improve her situation and I could only lower it, as I had no real property, only the smallest of fixed incomes, and was obliged to work for a living. And so she was persuaded to give me up."

"Those impediments have been removed," I reminded.

"Your situation has entirely changed."

"As have my feelings, of which only the faintest of memories remain with me. Though Miss Whitley and I did for a short time, share a mutual devotion, it has long passed. As is oft noted, time is a wondrous healer. She will have no place in my future."

"No matter," I replied, quite unforgiving. "I am sure we can find a promising candidate that will at once suit you and your aunt as well."

I looked around the street to find the source of a loud high-pitched laugh.

"Miss Temple. She comes with 10,000 pounds. Obviously sweet-tempered, lively, fond of a good laugh."

The lieutenant flinched at Miss Temple's jarring squeals. "You think I could ever feel affection for such a woman?"

"Well, *I* could not marry without love, but I am far from insisting that others share my scruples. But here is another lovely option. Consider the Widow Amesley."

I pointed to a proud, haughty woman of forty years, very elegantly dressed.

"I have always noticed that men are fonder of widows than they are of spinsters. And why not? Her husband left her with 20,000. Moreover, she will be a grateful and experienced wife."

"You are very kind," the lieutenant responded grimly.

A plump young woman of two and twenty years, familiar to me from the churchyard, was the next to capture my attention.

"Miss Darter. Only 5000 pounds, but look at her. That woman will bear children like a champion breeder. If you do not get six boys out of her, I will be much surprised."

The lieutenant looked decidedly ungrateful.

"You are difficult to please Lieutenant. I am afraid that brings us right back to Miss Whitley."

"That is no longer where my heart lies. Surely you must know that."

I spotted the lieutenant's brother approaching. Good. I required a reprieve both from the lieutenant's confusing and earnest denials and from my own lunacy.

"Good afternoon, Miss Austen," Dr. Barnes greeted. "I'm sorry to pull Frederick away, but we have both been summoned by our aunt to make some preparations to welcome ... our guest."

He glanced at me nervously. Now this truly *was* becoming unbearable. Even his brother knew enough of what was unfolding to pity me.

"I would not wish to cause you any delay. Good afternoon, gentlemen. My best regards to your *guest*."

I left without waiting a response. I was well and truly drained and wanted only peace from this self-inflicted torment. I headed back to the cottage, where talk of mutton joints, and foul weather, and smugglers, and the difficulty of finding a good dentist, were the only respite available to crowd out all wayward and dangerous thoughts. Thus I achieved some measure of escape. It would be of short enough duration. In two days' time, I was promised to dance with the lieutenant at the Assembly Room Ball. And I should finally lay eyes on the infamous Miss Alicia Whitley. I took up my pen up to return to worlds under my control.

Elizabeth Bennet and young Maria
Lucas peered out of the window at Miss De
Bourgh, a stunning beauty of one and

twenty, sitting in the carriage and conversing with Mr. Collins.

"Miss De Bourgh is beautiful, is she not?" Maria enthused.

"Yes, Mr. Darcy is most fortunate in his choice of wife," Elizabeth noted unhappily.

Hmmph. He *did* say that it had been six years since their involvement. And no one can remain a beauty forever.

Elizabeth Bennet and Maria Lucas peered out of the window at Miss De Bourgh, a somewhat plain looking young lady, though amiable enough.

"She's a very sweet-pleasant-looking girl, is she not?" Maria ventured.

"Oh, good enough for the likes of Mr. Darcy," Elizabeth declared.

It still did not satisfy.

Elizabeth Bennet and young Maria Lucas recoiled at the sight of Miss De Bourgh, the sickliest, homeliest creature either one of them had ever laid eyes upon.

"I am sure she looks much better when she is not feeling so poorly," Maria sympathized.

"I like her very much," Elizabeth exulted. "She will make a perfect wife for him."

With these happy visions floating in my head, I was comforted, and could anticipate the impending encounters with forbearance and calm.

CHAPTER TEN
THE GOOD LIE

The evening before the dance, my mother chided me for spending the entire afternoon away when I had known that Reverend Blackall was expected for tea and that he had expressed a particular wish to see me.

"I make promises to the Reverend and then I break them. Is it not a most effective way of communicating my regard for him?" I carelessly defended.

"Will you instruct *your* daughter on manners and duty, Mr. Austen?" my mother demanded.

Papa replied, "*My* daughter, is she? Poor motherless creature. Well, here is the sum total of my advice then. Reverend Blackall has more to materially recommend him than I ever did as a suitor. But I am perceptive enough to see that he will never be my son-in-law, and that no one should waste breath or hope in that misguided expectation. Still, we must not lose sight of the fact that he is a friend of Mrs. Lefroy's. Give him two dances, Jane. As a courtesy to *her*. And he will be out of our lives soon enough."

I grumbled my reluctant consent. The disaster was complete. Between the lieutenant, Miss Whitley, and Reverend Blackall, I had never anticipated a social engagement where no pleasure could be expected and every turn of the head was guaranteed to annoy and anguish. It felt much in common with entering battle, and indeed, that is how I should regard it. I must not allow myself to be overcome by the enemy, but to stand my ground, and to walk away from the battlefield unscathed. That will be my victory. Filled with resolve, I made sure that my ball gown was in readiness, secured Cassie's promise that she would remain close, and forced myself into a long but fitful sleep.

The Assembly Room was superbly adorned, reminding me very much of the ball room at Godmersham. It was the largest ball of the summer and all of Sidmouth's privileged and educated society was in attendance. It was easy to feel somewhat inconsequential in such a large crowd, which I regarded as an asset. Cassie and I sipped on glasses of wine and kept a watchful eye for any familiar faces.

"Slowly, Jane. Turn very, very slowly," Cassie whispered.

I obeyed with appropriate nonchalance, just in time to observe the arrival of Lieutenant Barnes. He had Mrs. Doherty on one arm, and Miss Whitley on the other, who was one of the loveliest young women I had ever beheld. Of course she was. Of course.

It was under ten minutes later that the dancing began and the lieutenant quickly made his way to my side.

"Miss Jane. I have come to claim the first two dances."

"Lieutenant, those arrangements were made before you knew you were to have ... a guest. Under the circumstances, I am more than happy to release you from the obligation."

"I have no desire to be released."

It could not be avoided. The lieutenant led me to the dance floor, where I soon noticed, we were under Mrs. Doherty's disapproving gaze. We lined up with the other couples. There was enough reunion in the dance to allow for some brief conversation.

"I trust Miss Whitley's visit is going well," I prodded.

"It is always good to see old friends. Though we meet on very different terms than our former acquaintance."

Miss Whitley and Dr. Barnes were dancing nearby.

"She is the very picture of elegance. Definitely not a naval wife. It is well that she waited until you could secure your inheritance."

"It was secured at the cost of a dear cousin's life," the lieutenant reprimanded.

"I am sorry," I stammered. "Truly. At times, I am completely abandoned by all civilized impulses. Will you ... can you ...?"

"You are entirely forgiven, Miss Jane. And now, the next apology will be in your hands, for I have no doubt there will be a steady exchange of offenses."

I was put at ease, despite myself. Why could I not simply be contented with his friendship alone? How best to reconcile myself to this disheartening change of circumstances, when his every word and look prolonged my feelings? I required a cold dose of reality.

"I shall expect an introduction," I declared.

"Then you shall have it," he conceded.

Excellent. It was vastly preferable to tormenting myself

over her imagined virtues. I could only now hope to find some glaring follies or inadequacies that would make me pity the lieutenant or despise him. Our dance was concluded in silence; apprehension on his part, perhaps, and an excess of anticipation on mine.

After the lieutenant left me, I watched him dance with Miss Whitley. A handsome couple, no one could deny. He was courteous, but grave. I could imagine that her refusal some six years ago was still weighing upon his mind. Had he not said himself that he did not wish to be loved only for his impending fortune? And had not Miss Whitley and her family only evidenced a change of heart when the lieutenant gained his inheritance? I was thoroughly prepared to dislike her.

It was but another ten minutes when the opportunity arose. The lieutenant led Miss Whitley straight to where Cassie and I were standing. Out of the corner of my eye, I saw Mrs. Doherty gesturing Dr. Barnes over, to intervene, presumably. The lieutenant cordially presided over the introductions.

"I am very pleased to meet you both. Lieutenant Barnes and Dr. Barnes have spoken very highly of you," Miss Whitley smiled.

"They have both been very kind," Cassie responded.

It would have been a polite convention to return the compliment and to let Miss Whitley know that she was also highly regarded by our mutual friends, but I could not exert the effort.

"I hope you are enjoying your visit, Miss Whitley," I managed.

"Oh, yes. I look forward to a highly enjoyable fortnight. Mrs. Doherty has been the most gracious hostess. She is all kindness and hospitality. But then, you are acquainted with her, and have no doubt, seen this for yourself."

The lieutenant had the good sense to grimace at this false assumption. Dr. Barnes arrived to join us, relieving me of the obligation to respond.

"I cannot believe you all would squander such excellent music. Miss Austen, will you join me?"

Dr. Barnes offered his arm to Cassie. "And Frederick, please go to Aunt Doherty. She had an urgent matter to discuss with you."

As Dr. Barnes led Cassie to the dance floor, the lieutenant glanced uneasily between Miss Whitley and myself.

"Be assured, Lieutenant, I shall take good care of Miss Whitley," I urged.

The lieutenant bowed and made his reluctant exit. Miss Whitley was at my mercy, and I was not feeling particularly merciful.

"Has it been long since you last saw Lieutenant Barnes?" I began.

"We have not regularly been in one another's company these past six years."

"Since you refused him?" I prompted.

She was unnerved. "Yes I see you have become a trusted friend. I did refuse him many years ago, at my family's insistence."

"Perfectly understandable. As the only things he had to recommend him were a degree from Cambridge and a clergyman's income. It was not a grand offering."

"It did not trouble me. He had such fine qualities that I did believe that a modest style of living would be very acceptable."

"But ..." I prodded.

"His lack of property was not acceptable," she admitted. "Not to my father."

"Well, you cannot fault a man for looking after his daughter's best interests," I offered disingenuously.

"The fault, I believe, was mine. My father was entitled to his feelings, but matters of the heart should not be subjected to blind obedience. I do regret my refusal, Miss Austen. I truly do. And I am so grateful that Frederick is not a resentful or unforgiving man."

"No indeed. And *now* he is a most worthy prospect," I pronounced.

"As he ever was," Miss Whitley noted regretfully.

Our conversation moved into other arenas. Miss Whitley had quite a broad appreciation of theatre. She spoke most affectionately of her sisters and brother; and she had an admirable grasp of the consequences of war, well beyond the disruption of her supply of French fashion and French wine. She was exceedingly pleasant and reasonably intelligent, and try as I might, I searched at length for satisfying flaws, but with no success.

Dr. Barnes and Cassie rejoined us. It was the briefest of reunions, for we were immediately set upon by Reverend Blackall, who required introductions, and then anxiously inquired whether I could join him for the next two dances. I had no ready excuse and was obliged to submit. He was a tolerable dancer, but the steps required so much of his concentration, that I was subjected to very little conversation. Glancing at the sidelines, I did notice the lieutenant watching me with great interest. Why did he not focus his attentions on Miss Whitley and end this confusion?

As our two dances ended, I suspected that the Reverend

intended to stay close by my side, which I would not allow. As we approached Cassie, I mentioned my concern that she might feel neglected. Here was a chance to impress me with his gallantry. The Reverend engaged Cassie for the next two dances, and I was able to slip outside the Assembly Room, take in the fresh air and night sky, and remove myself from any more demanding encounters.

I watched the many arrivals and small number of early departures. I was more than ready to go home myself, as all the evening's objectives had been achieved. But for appearances' sake, another full hour of entertainment was required. I could consume a quarter of that time by slowly circumnavigating the building, which I proceeded to do.

I returned to the ballroom quite refreshed, and happy that so little time remained before Cassie and I could make a respectable exit. I saw that Cassie was being held captive in conversation with the Reverend, but I took care that they should not see *me*. After all, Cassie was of such easy temperament that she might actually be enjoying the Reverend's company. Or at least, was little pained by it. I had just spotted a few familiar faces from the churchyard, and resolved to be sociable, when the music took a turn. The unmistakable chords of a waltz filled the air, and there was a discernible reaction in the room, flutters of both excitement and disapproval. Now this would be well worth watching.

"Miss Jane, may I have this waltz?" the lieutenant surprised me, appearing out of nowhere.

This was entirely too much attentiveness. Surely both Mrs. Doherty and Miss Whitley would take notice.

"We have already danced, sir. You do me too much honour."

But he held out his hand insistently, and I was led to the

floor. He never released my hand, but encircled my waist with his other limb and drew me closer. His hands were so warm and his body was so close. I struggled to maintain my composure.

"Are you enjoying your evening, Miss Jane?"

"Very much. I was particularly happy to make Miss Whitley's acquaintance. She is sweet-tempered, and obviously quite beautiful," I asserted.

"She is exemplary," the lieutenant noted grudgingly.

"You can look forward to an enviable inheritance and the loveliest of wives. I am happy for you. It is what you deserve, and I wish you both very happy."

"I did not grow up with the expectation of this inheritance. And when it was offered to me, I had no idea that it should be so unacceptably encumbered. I will not allow my wife to be chosen for me."

"But she was your own choice," I reminded.

"Perhaps it is possible to revive a fire from last night's embers. But not from a flame extinguished six years ago. Those feelings have gone, and now I see more clearly, never had a solid foundation."

"Wealth and security are a very solid foundation," I countered.

"Whatever the consequences, I shall insist on love. Love that I scarcely believed in but one month ago."

His meaning was clear. But unfathomable. Who could treasure *me* above such security, such peace of mind, such guarantee of ease? And with such beauty thrown into the bargain! No, this was not a rational man, this man swirling me about the ballroom, jumbling my own power of reason, and threatening to pull me back into the paradise of hope.

That was our last dance together, but doubtless there

would have been more, had I not forcefully urged Cassie into an early departure. I was in sore need of a retreat to safety and relative solitude. And pen.

Marianne Dashwood and John Willoughby enjoyed a romantic waltz.

"I do not give two straws if I should lose my inheritance," Willoughby declared. "Marrying you will make me the happiest man in the world."

"As long as we can be together, it matters not what deprivations must be endured," Marianne gushed.

"Certainly not. Love will sustain us through every trial," Willoughby agreed.

"We shall barely notice the absence of unnecessary luxuries. We do not require hunters or even a carriage," Marianne mused.

"Hunters? Indeed. No. They have been a most enjoyable thing certainly. But not essential to happiness. No. Indeed not. And a carriage ..." Willoughby's voice faltered. "A carriage is a very fine thing. Its absence can certainly create difficulties."

"We shall walk. Our neighbors can oblige us with a ride from time to time. And I am sure we can do with only one servant. No need for a manservant or a gardener. Darling, can you not take care of the gardening duties?"

"What? You mean chopping wood!?"

*"Our felicity will blind us to all
hardship and discomfort. Oh, Willoughby.
How happy we shall be."*

*Willoughby pulled Marianne close, so
that she would not see his panic-stricken
change of heart.*

Cassie finished undressing and glanced at my writing as she climbed into bed.

"That is not *First Impressions*," she observed.

"No. I had a few alterations for *Elinor and Marianne*. It wanted a few touches of reality."

I climbed into bed, praying for the strength to do what so obviously needed to be done.

I awoke with a plan. I cannot say whether it was a good plan. But I needed to shield myself from the lieutenant's blind attachment, and to protect him as well. He could not see the future as clearly as I. I must sacrifice him. And he would go on to lead a prosperous and happy life. I would take comfort in that. For it would take great resolve on my part to execute and uphold this plan. But there was nothing else to be done. I had only to await opportunity.

It was my intention to create some pretext to visit the lieutenant sometime in the next few days. It was easily done. I still had many books of his in my possession. With a heavy heart, I was again drawn to the waves, knowing that today they would mirror my dark mood. The air was cold and blustery, and the gray sky threatened rain. The waves crashed ominously, warning all to keep their distance. There was so much noise about, that I did not hear the lieutenant approach.

"Miss Jane. You spend as much time on the waves as

myself."

"Lieutenant ... I am glad for this chance to speak to you," I began.

"Last night ... I hope I was able to make you understand ... to make my feelings clear." His voice rose to overcome the roar of the waves. "I have come to ask you a question, Miss Jane. Of greatest importance to my future happiness."

There was no time to delay. I could not let him ask it.

"You have come to ask my advice on marriage. I am happy to oblige. You should marry Miss Whitley. It is the course of action that will bring about the greatest good of all concerned."

His ardent expression became stern. "This is no time for jest," he warned. "We must speak plainly."

"You are most fortunate that your marriage will not cause your family any distress," I added hurriedly. "I only wish I could say the same of my own marriage."

"Your own ...?"

"Yes," I managed with feigned calm. "I have had to keep the news of my own engagement a secret from my entire family."

The lieutenant drew back, examining me with numb shock. "Engagement!?"

"My father relies on my company so. He will be inconsolable at the thought of my absence. And my mother's frequent illnesses ... she requires nursing constantly. So I know not when or how I shall be able to share the news with them. But there you are lucky. Your news will be warmly received."

The rain began to fall. All the better, to bring this dreadful performance to a quick conclusion.

"You are engaged!!"

"Yes. But I beg you not to share this information with anyone, for the reasons I have already stated."

Perhaps there had been some small corner of my mind that doubted his true feelings. That believed that the loss of me would prove to be an annoyance, or a blow to his pride, but no real wound. But there was no mistaking the fury and the pain in his eyes as he grabbed me tightly about the shoulders.

"Why did you not tell me you were spoken for? Do you have a heart of stone, or are you just completely blind?" he demanded.

By now, the sky was pelting us with heavy drops, and I could clearly speak no more. He released me and backed away, shaking his head. He looked upwards and gave his face a cold punishing bath. Did he think the rain could dampen his misery? Returning his gaze to me, he gestured furiously at me and towards a path that led back to the streets, practical even in his anguish. And then he was gone.

It was a shock to see how he suffered but, surely I protected him from irreparable losses and regrets. Why then, did the blinding bolts of lightning and the angry cracks of thunder reproach me with their judgment? The harsh rain and bitter wind echoed unmistakable censure.

I felt the certainty drain out of me. I had succeeded, but felt no triumph. My knees buckled underneath me, and I sank to the drenched earth. I was well-positioned for prayer, but what could I possibly hope to pray for?

CHAPTER ELEVEN
ALL TRUTHS REVEALED

My parents knew not what to make of my changeful mood. I made continual inquiries as to the date of our departure from Sidmouth. I who loved the seaside and who dreaded Bath. My mother's relatives were in Bath. Surely we could stay with them while our renovations were being finished. Had we not trespassed on Mr. Shaw's hospitality for far too long?

I could not sit still long enough to write, and was obliged to invent tasks for myself that would remove me from the cottage. I did my best to accomplish only one mission at a time, for if there were two things to be done, the second was most usefully reserved for a second expedition. On this particular afternoon, I sought to replenish the bars of soap that the Austen family had depleted in Mr. Shaw's home. It was a task well-structured for lengthiness. For there were countless stores with the same general product of differing prices and fragrances, and I was able to vanquish a considerable amount of time in this manner.

As I came out of one shop, I nearly collided with

Reverend Blackall.

"I beg your pardon, Miss Austen. I am so glad I was able to catch up with you. Your parents said I might be able to find you here."

"That was thoughtful of them," I grumbled. "I shall be sure to thank them for it."

I looked about me for some means of escape. Far from it, I spotted a worse danger in the form of Lieutenant Frederick Barnes, at quite a distance from us, but most certainly looking in our direction. Whatever task he had at hand had come to a standstill. His attention was upon us and did not waver. At once, I had a recollection of being under the lieutenant's gaze while dancing at the Assembly Ball. Whenever I had had occasion to be with the Reverend in a public sphere, I could admit to feeling somewhat mortified lest our relationship might be misconstrued. But in an instant, I saw that this misunderstanding could work to my advantage.

I asked the Reverend if he would accompany me for the reminder of my tasks, and then join me for a cup of tea ... an invitation that was eagerly received. I took the Reverend's arm and we continued to the next shop. Our backs were now to the lieutenant, but I had no doubt we were still under surveillance. So be it. I finally had reason to be grateful to the Reverend, and resolved to listen in rapt attention to whatever direction his ramblings took.

It proved a taller order than I could have imagined. Our tea was interminable. The Reverend was inexplicably fixated on the issue of colour. He wanted to describe the interior of his parsonage, so that I could imagine it clearly. He was able to point to the dress on this woman, and the bonnet on that one, and the flower design upon our teacups, all to help me understand how artfully decorated his walls were, and how pleasing the combinations would be to a discerning woman of taste. I confess, I may be sensitive to colour, but I am not enthralled by it, and I was anxious to steer the conversation in another direction.

"I hope the colours of our new house in Bath will be to our satisfaction. It is difficult to rent a house, not having seen it, but my uncle has assured us it is well located."

"Oh, certainly," the Reverend replied, anxious to please. "But it seems unlikely that it will be an extended stay for either of the Austen daughters, for such charming young ladies should certainly not be long under your parents' roof."

"They do depend on us, as they are both advanced in years," I deflected. "I cannot foresee ever leaving them."

The Reverend smiled warmly. "Your sense of duty does you credit. A most desirable quality in a … a young lady."

Was there a man alive more impervious to insult? I so wanted to tell the Reverend that I should never marry him, in terms that even *he* could not fail to understand. But it was far too soon for that blow. Not while I still needed him. Not while the lieutenant was still in Sidmouth. Still, there was no need to prolong my ordeal, for surely the streets must be clear of danger by this time. When my hasty fabrication of a headache only created a determination in the Reverend to see me home safely, I had to say that, in addition, I had promised a visit to Martha. And so he was obliged to allow my departure.

After that afternoon, I quickly concluded I should be much safer by remaining close to home. Apparently, Sidmouth was not large enough to avoid these frequent and trying encounters. And so I busied myself about the garden, weaned through Mr. Shaw's anemic book collection, and tried to win my family over to the idea of an early departure.

Mama's stomach took a turn for the worst, and she became determined to call Dr. Barnes for his assessment. I was sure it was a minor complaint, but she was insistent. I was somewhat resentful that her peace of mind should be gratified at the expense of mine. But I could not explain to them why I was loathe to see Dr. Barnes. And so he came.

He proved to be a soothing practitioner. His comforting reassurances brought Mama as much cure as the medicine he left behind. He accepted an invitation to tea, and provided a satisfying spark of conversation. All the more needed, as my troubled thoughts robbed me of any ability to be sociable. My lack of speech was noticed by all, but thankfully, no one was so unkind as to draw attention to it.

I did escort Dr. Barnes to his carriage. We were both weighed down with books that needed to be restored to the Barnes family library.

"Give your family my best regards, Dr. Barnes. And Miss Whitley too, of course."

The doctor regarded me with some hesitation and far too much compassion for my comfort.

"You are very kind, Miss Austen. You made a very favorable impression on Miss Whitley. I am sure she would be happy to make your further acquaintance."

"I was equally impressed, Dr. Barnes. She seemed an ideal sort of young lady, who will be admired in any circle she finds herself in."

The doctor nodded. "When she and Frederick formed their attachment all those years ago, I did think him the luckiest man in the world. In fact, I was rather envious. Though I could not envy his subsequent heartache. But he did manage to rally, and now they are thrown together once more, and may well revive their former attachment. Although I am not entirely sure that he is capable of recovering the same depth of affection. Perhaps it is a height of feeling bestowed only to youth."

Could I take any comfort in these revelations? It was enough that comfort was intended, and I bid the doctor a grateful farewell.

◇◇◇

Some days later, I returned to the cottage with Mama after another invigorating session in the bathing machine. Cassie led me back to our bedroom, seemingly intent on revealing some confidence.

"Now, I do not mean to make you angry, Jane," Cassie began.

"I cannot imagine such a thing is even possible," I reassured her. "But by all means, confess. And we shall see if my opinion is in need of revision."

Cassie paced the room and I could only wonder at what was to come.

"Lieutenant Barnes stopped by while you were out."

"Did he? That is … most unexpected. What was his purpose?"

"Oh, Jane. To see you, of course. But he had to content himself with speaking of you."

"And what had he to say?" I marveled.

"I do not think the lieutenant can be as attached to Miss Whitley as you were led to believe. He was in the lowest of spirits. And Jane, he was under the astonishing impression that you and Reverend Blackall were on exceedingly intimate footing. Well, you can imagine how entertained I was by that notion. There is no one in the Austen family who can be in doubt regarding your feelings for the Reverend. Are you not astounded?"

"I suppose he has seen us together on a few occasions and misconstrued," I evaded.

"Hmm. I am sure there is more to it than that. Jane, what did you say to him?"

"Never mind that. What did *you* say to him," I demanded.

"I said I believed him to be very much mistaken, and he apologized if he was inflicting any distress, but ventured that I simply might not be in your confidence in this matter."

"You were not able to dissuade him?" I inquired hopefully.

"No," Cassie sighed.

"Well, I cannot blame you for any of this … and you need not have worried that I should be angry."

"You have not heard all," Cassie admitted most reluctantly.

"No? What more?"

"You have to understand, Jane. It pained me to see him so low. And I only wanted to raise his spirits. To take him away from his troubles."

"And you did what?" I inquired.

"I gave him your manuscript to read."

It took a couple of seconds for the magnitude of the crime to sink in. Time enough for Cassie to back away to as distant a spot as possible. Well-advised, for my anger had never boiled with such fervor. Were we men, we should have come to blows. How had my privacy been snatched away from me so cruelly? That story was mine alone, not to be shared outside the family circle. Certainly not in the state that it was in. So unpolished and so revealing! And he was reading it right at this moment.

"Jane, your story has entertained me so greatly. I was certain it should do him good. And he will be sure to return it in a few days' time."

"He will return it this instant, and I shall deal with you when I return," I pronounced through gritted teeth.

I stormed out of the room. I could not even decide how severely Cassie should be punished, and had to put that matter in secondary place. The Barnes' home was about an hour's brisk walk from our cottage. It was a good amount of time to ponder all manner of verbal assaults, for my fury certainly did not dissipate. Though Cassie had committed the greater offense, the lieutenant should have known he was engaged in the most unpardonable intrusion. It was much like opening another's diary, or eavesdropping on a bedroom conversation. Did he hope to mortify me? To punish me for my engagement revelation? By the time I arrived, I was determined he should receive a lambasting of the highest order. A verbal flogging. Yes, that is exactly what he deserved.

When the manservant announced me and showed me into the drawing room, I was greeted with the sight of my manuscript balanced on the lieutenant's knee. He rose immediately.

"How dare you? That is private property and meant for the eyes of me and my family alone," I ranted.

"You have borrowed much reading from me these last few weeks, Miss Jane. Are you truly unwilling to extend me the same courtesy?"

"It is not the same. It was an unpardonable violation."

"But it was your sister who invited me to look it over,"

he defended.

"You should both be exceedingly ashamed of yourselves."

"Do not try to distract me from your own misbehavior. It is *I* who should be angry at you."

"What?" I sputtered.

"*You* have engaged in the worst and most deceitful of all falsehoods. For did you not promise me, did you not swear to me, that you were completely devoid of talent?"

I was perplexed; was this some scheme to divert me from the matter at hand?

"As you know, I took the greatest comfort in your absence of talent, happy in the knowledge I would not have to waste energy or time on admiring another young lady's skills. But there is such an abundance of talent here. I have lost an entire afternoon to it. And I have but little hope for my evening."

He was in earnest; he was truly entertained. By my writing! I felt a flush of gratification that I had not felt in many, many years. Not since I was cheered by my young schoolhouse audience. It is one thing to please an easy indulgent audience of family. But an outsider … with an intelligent and discerning mind? I confess, I had always hoped my stories might hold up to public scrutiny. Was it really worthy of such praise?

"Come Lieutenant. It can hardly stand next to Miss Edgeworth's novels," I challenged.

"I cannot agree. It contains such wit, such humour, as to rank with the best of its kind. It is delightful."

My resentment was defenseless against such a barrage of accolades. Such moments in life were rare, and I was suddenly quite ready to sacrifice my anger. I sat down on the couch and he joined me. My precious writing had finally encountered the world and I could not resist.

"Which parts did you like best?" I solicited, with an attempt at indifference.

The next half-hour passed in very pleasant fashion, indeed. He laughed where he was meant to laugh. And he took notice of the sections I had labored over at great length. Of course, I had to grant him the privilege of reading the remainder of the story. He swore on his honour as a servant of the Royal Navy that the document would be safely restored to me. How completely unexpectedly this encounter had unfolded. Perhaps we should end our acquaintance on good terms, after all. Despite my protests, he ordered a carriage to see me home. Well, perhaps there was no harm in accepting it, as he did owe me an apology. I smiled to remember his observation that we should constantly be trading offenses and apologies. And so we parted in relative peace.

During my twenty minutes in the carriage, I could only regret my delay in dealing with Cassie. She had acted so badly that she should suffer the brunt of my fury. Instead, I had set the confrontation aside and lost my heat of rage as a consequence. It was truly a pity, for I should not like her to think that such traitorous acts would be so easily excused. So I tried to remember and recover some small amount of outrage, but my dark efforts were smothered by the praise still ringing in my ears. Very well then. Perhaps I would have to forgive her. Particularly since I was bursting to share the lieutenant's generous appreciation.

I showed Cassie no leniency during supper, and refused her every overture. It was not until we retired for bed that I was compelled to momentarily relent.

"Your breach of trust was unpardonable. However, I have matters on which I desire to speak, and therefore, I will call a truce of twenty minutes duration," I announced. "Do not mistake it for forgiveness."

Cassie nodded. With gratitude, I should hope.

I continued. "He ... enjoyed it. Truly enjoyed it. He was most entertained, or so he led me to believe."

"It is a delightful story, as I have told you many times," Cassie responded. "And your brothers ... have they not told you time and again how greatly they enjoy your stories?"

"Family may be relied upon for affection, but not truth."

"And the lieutenant's opinion?" Cassie inquired.

"It did resemble sincerity. Somewhat like myself, he is not handicapped by an excess of manners. So, I was inclined to take him at his word."

"His manners are perfectly fine, but I am glad that thought provides further reassurance."

I had come to the point that I wished to deliver with as much nonchalance as I could muster. "He said he preferred my story to Maria Edgeworth's. Now there he has gone too far. For thousands of people have paid money to acquire her works."

"Not a soul in the world would have spent any money on Mrs. Edgeworth had she not troubled to offer her work for publication." Cassie smiled encouragingly at me.

I climbed into bed, satisfied. "Our truce is up. We are no longer on speaking terms."

I heard her sigh with exasperation as I settled down for a gratifying recollection of the day's compliments.

◇◇◇

Two days passed, and all paths seemed destined to cross again in the churchyard. Cassie and I waited patiently while our parents went on a series of exchanges with their elderly peers. I did expect the lieutenant to stop by for a few pleasantries. But what I did *not* expect was that he should find himself deep in conversation with Reverend Blackall! I watched in amazement for some fifteen minutes. What could be the meaning of this?

"Cassie. This is a most unlikely pairing, is it not?"

"Perhaps Reverend Blackall seeks advice on some matter," Cassie speculated.

"The Reverend does not strike me as a man who takes advice. Certainly not from anyone other than his patroness. His opinions and pride are rigidly impervious to the concept of improvement," I argued.

What was the real purpose of this conversation?

"Are you still eager to depart from Bath?" Cassie wondered.

"Well, do you not think we have been here quite long enough? There are, after all, so few diversions here."

"Few in number, yes. But how many *diversions* does a young lady need?" Cassie noted slyly, with raised eyebrow.

"You are not yet back in my good graces. Do not provoke me any further."

Cassie smiled. "Good afternoon, Lieutenant."

I whirled around to face the man himself.

"Good afternoon to you both. Miss Jane, it is a fine day, is it not? Perhaps you would enjoy a walk along the water?"

I started to protest that Cassie and I already had fixed plans for the afternoon. But when I turned about to secure her accord, she had vanished entirely. She really could be too infuriating. I steeled myself for a session of banal civilities. Or better still, perhaps he had further comment on my manuscript. And so we set out for the beach.

"I have had an interesting discussion with Reverend Blackall," he began.

His sharp eyes examined my face, on high alert for the slightest reaction.

"Indeed?"

"Yes, and I could not help but notice that he spoke very highly and very fondly of you."

"Oh."

"And I was reminded that I have seen the two of you on a number of occasions," the lieutenant continued. "You have already given me your confidence. Now please tell me all. Is your secret engagement to Reverend Blackall?"

I knew that this was the impression I had hoped to give, but I had not thought such a direct confirmation would be required. Still, though it was a lie of great enormity, I was unlikely to be found out, as both Austen and Barnes families were so soon to depart from Sidmouth, and should probably never hear of one another ever again.

"Yes, if you must know. I am engaged to marry Reverend Blackall."

The lieutenant stepped quickly into my path and turned to face me. "Hah! Jane Austen, that is the last time I will permit you to lie to me. I cannot suppose for a moment you would devote yourself to such a man."

"He is an honourable man. A man of humility," I argued.

"Much like Mr. Collins. Though I never dreamt to encounter such a man in the flesh. 'Have self-importance and humility ever resided so peculiarly in one skin?' Those are *your* words."

"That is a wholly fictitious character. It has nothing to
do with Reverend Blackall. I have nothing but the highest ...
He and I are very much..."

The lieutenant raised an incredulous eyebrow, daring
me to continue the lie. I sighed, and hung my head in defeat.
The ruse was uncovered.

"Why? When you knew why I came to find you that
day?"

"Because I saw that you could not curb your own
foolish impulses. And so the job fell to me. You cannot
disregard what your aunt has to offer."

"I care not," he replied, most emphatically.

"You have given it very little thought," I scolded. "And
you underestimate life's difficulties. My father worked long
and hard and with honour. But these last five years, our
circumstances have sunk lower and lower. If we did not have
free hospitality here in Sidmouth, we should be hard-pressed
to cover expenses. Paper and tea and sugar and buttons ...
there is nothing that has not been placed on careful rations.
People with property are shielded from such indignities."

The lieutenant wanted to speak, but I would not let him.

"When my father dies, which I hate to think on, my
sister and I will be recipients of charity, which will sting,
even though it come from loving brothers. Think of what
you will owe to your children, for they are likely to arrive in
large numbers. Think of the ease and freedom you can
bestow on your family. You cannot turn your back on this
opportunity."

"Am I to place such security above the demands of my
heart?"

"Miss Whitley will be the best of wives. When she
refused you, she was but eighteen, a very young woman,

under the close influence of her parents. Surely you cannot be so unforgiving as to deny her predicament. Is your pride so unyielding? ... If you let that pride stand between you and certain happiness, I will always remember you as a fool."

I had stunned him into silence and doubt. He searched my eyes intently to uncover my true meaning. I could not stay and allow him to argue, nor allow him to hope. I turned and barreled resolutely away from him. It was done.

But I could not head home, and the waves were no longer my refuge. I found myself at Martha's door, in need of soothing comfort and a strong shoulder. She listened, she consoled, and she understood. Martha was overly familiar with a multitude of life's harsh lessons, particularly where money was concerned. She had had much occasion to reflect on poverty and an uncertain future, on the merciless workings of the marriage economy, the blessings of good fortune, and how miserly those blessings had been handed out. And she had witnessed, as had I, many marriages born out of passion that had lost all affection after twenty ensuing years of hardship.

"He would regret it one day. And I could never bear to see that regret in his eyes," I sighed.

Martha nodded and held me close. She was doctor and cure all in one. I knew that I had hit my lowest, and there was nothing to do now but to mend. I had done it once before. I simply had to remember how.

◇◇◇

The next morning, I received the welcome news that a date had finally been set for our departure, ten days hence. It was a great deal of time to fill, but a comforting deadline all the same. Most of our obligations in those final days would be of a mundane sort. But there was one social engagement that we had agreed to several weeks earlier: a ball we had been invited to on the strength of an introduction from Mama's relations in Bath. We could not snub them, no matter how ill-matched my mood was for dancing and sociability. I could best look upon it as an effective means of passing time; both the event itself and any preparation. The entire Austen family was in attendance, accompanied by Mr. Shaw, who I believe was already a bit forlorn over our impending absence. He had also promised to exploit his Sidmouth acquaintance to secure a few introductions and dances for Cassie and myself, but he could not have known how indifferent I was on that matter.

The evening passed slowly, and before long, the ballroom became too warm. I knew I needed cool fresh air to revive me. I walked out and around to the side of the building, where I had easy view of the elegant scene within. I was much more content to be an observer tonight, unburdened with the pretense of gaiety and enjoyment. I could appreciate the dance as one appreciates a painting. It was indeed, a pretty sight, and I wanted nothing more from the evening.

"There are few things so refreshing as the night air," Lieutenant Barnes startled me from behind. "Some say it brings on chills and fever, but I have never believed it."

"Lieutenant, I did not expect to see you here. I … hope you are well."

"Very well, thank you. I have spent the last few days enjoying the company of my family and our guest."

"Oh, how is Miss Whitley?" I inquired reluctantly.

"She is sweet, and good-hearted, and charming. Very

charming. And I have finally arrived at a decision that I hope will meet with your approval."

So there it was. I knew that he would come to his senses. It was just as I had hoped. In fact, I had almost fully contrived it. And still I shied away from hearing it.

"My family and I are leaving for Bath next Thursday. In truth, there is so much packing to do, I really should not have come tonight." I backed away from him.

"You will not ask me what decision I have arrived at." The lieutenant observed. "Most uncharacteristic reserve on your part. But I intend to tell you."

"There is no need, Lieutenant. None at all. Now, if you will excuse me, I must return to my family."

I turned to depart, but not before seeing the annoyed bewilderment covering his features. This was a final moment for he and I; I owed him this courtesy. I turned back.

"That was most uncivil of me. Particularly since you are only acting as I advised you. Tell me your news, Lieutenant. And let us be done."

"Miss Austen. It has been my great misfortune to lose my heart to a woman so rude, so uncivil, so filled with obstinacy and impertinence that I can only beg the Heavens to look down and have mercy on me. And I mean to ask for her hand. Very, very soon. That is my news."

Who could have believed that such a man existed? Before the expectations of society, he refused to bow. That he should prize me ... me of all people. I, who see too much and say too much. I, who lost all faith in true devotion. I was penniless. It did not matter. I was myself, and for this man, that was all I needed to be.

I could doubt no longer. His heart was steady. His devotion was unshakeable. And I could not help but feel the truth of my own heart. The deafening truth. It was I who had said that one should never turn one's back on the gift of a great inheritance, and here I had been on the verge of denying a far more precious gift.

"This news will not sit well with your aunt," I finally uttered.

"Aunt Doherty may dispose of her wealth as she sees fit. Andrew would be a most worthy recipient. Although I hope he does not abandon his medicine. And should he require a lovely and sweet-tempered and charming mistress for his estate, I think I know the perfect candidate."

"You are generous! Can Miss Whitley really be that resilient?"

The lieutenant shrugged. "I wish her well. I truly do."

"All right then. Now tell me, how do you propose to support your wife at the level of mild deprivation to which she has become accustomed."

"Well, I was obliged to give up my parish, and to a very worthy gentleman. I should never try to reclaim it. Still, I *do* have a small annual income from an uncle on my father's side. It is but four hundred pounds."

Well, that was cheering news. "Enough for a cook," I noted.

"And we have a family property in Lyme. Currently being occupied by tenants. But with a few months' notice and some assistance, they can be transferred elsewhere. It is a modest size, not unlike the home your family has stayed in here in Sidmouth. It does have a library, which is small, but receives excellent light. Well-suited for a novelist."

"Is there a novelist in residence there?"

"Not at present ... Jane..."

He drew closer and I was obliged to turn my back to

him, lest I burst into tears. I felt his hands clasp me about the waist and draw me back until I was resting against him. He started to sway very gently to the melody of the music escaping from the ballroom.

"Sir, if this is a waltz, I am facing in the wrong direction," I chided mildly.

"New dances must be invented from time to time, and who better Jane, than you and I?"

I turned around, tears threatening to spill over, and found myself engulfed in the warmest most heartfelt embrace I could ever have imagined possible.

CHAPTER TWELVE
WAITING IN BATH

How is one day so unfathomably different than the day before? That a bleak Friday morning should be followed by a luminous Saturday evening, and a Sunday where devotion and gratitude were truly in order. Frederick (for I may enjoy that familiarity now) and I spent the morning sermon in silent communion, sitting side by side. I could feel his thoughts, for we were at last, in perfect accord. There were but three days until his departure. What a small amount of time to savour one another's company. After the service, Frederick and his brother were invited to join the Austens for tea. Mrs. Doherty and Miss Whitley were conspicuously absent.

By mutual consent, Frederick and I slowed down our stride until we had achieved a wide swath of privacy. I knew that Miss Whitley had left for her home two days previously. But where was his aunt?

"Aunt Doherty is feeling a bit under the weather, as she received some news recently that did not sit well with her ... constitution."

"Do not tell me I must take responsibility for sending that good woman to an early grave," I mused, unrepentant. "But ... you will think me heartless."

Not wanting me to feel too badly, he had a confession of his own.

"When I was young, I thought Aunt Doherty was a witch. And I knew not how she made it alive through the Inquisition."

Such wickedness on a Sunday; we were both irrepressibly amused. Our impending separation removed all restraint.

"Your brother seemed a bit downcast today, did he not?"

"He is somewhat burdened by guilt," Frederick explained. "But I expect him to make a fast recovery, and to reconcile himself to his good fortune, soon enough. He likes you, Jane. He is certainly an ally."

"I like him too, very much. But I have yet to meet your parents, and I do not know what they will make of me."

"My mother will find you delightful ... without question," he predicted confidently.

"Ah, but your father will detest me."

"I said nothing of the kind," he sputtered.

"It is the omission that speaks volumes, Lieutenant," I teased.

"I must admit, his tastes can be narrow. But I will assure him that you improve on acquaintance."

"Oh, really? Like oysters?" I scoffed.

"Exactly like an oyster," he agreed.

"A kinder lover should have compared me to the pearl inside."

"I think the irritating grain of sand that precedes the

pearl might be more apropos."

I drew back in mock fury. This was not the love that I had read about in books, honey sweet and overflowing with ardent declarations. It was far, far more satisfying. It was real. It was ours.

Later that afternoon, after tea with my family, I walked him to the gate. He pulled a tiny box from the pocket of his uniform.

"Please accept this smallest of tokens, Miss Jane."

I saw how anxiously he wanted to please, and that was all the gift I required. Inside, the box, I was amazed to find the lovely pearl edged pendant he had selected for his mother.

"Sir, you rob your mother," I stammered.

"You caught me unawares that day in the jewelry shop. But I was happy to get your opinion on it. For it was never intended for any other."

He might just as well have kissed me, so deeply could I feel his heart reach out to mine.

Frederick came to visit on the morning of his departure. My parents had observed the two of us these past three days with many a raised eyebrow and a curious look, but spared me any questions. They and Cassie joined me at Frederick's carriage to say goodbye.

"It was a pleasure to meet all of you and I hope to see you … soon," the lieutenant conveyed.

"Certainly, for everyone says that the war is almost concluded. And we should be delighted to see you again," Mama offered graciously.

"Indeed," Papa added, "We shall look forward to it. Good journey to you."

"Goodbye, Lieutenant," Cassie concluded.

The lieutenant bowed, and Cassie gently pulled our parents back towards the cottage. Frederick gestured towards his manservant.

"Norton, could you carry that box inside?"

Norton pulled out a heavy gift-wrapped rectangular box.

"A small gift," Frederick explained.

He reached for my hand and kissed it tenderly. What soft warm lips. Surely as soft as my own. What delights were in store! I knew that my family was watching from the house's entrance and I was glad of it. He was a worthy addition to any family and I knew that he would be nothing but welcome.

"Now, I have told you my family and I suffer when we are not able to hear from my brothers. You must promise to be the most diligent of correspondents," I demanded.

"Any time we touch shore, I promise to have a letter in readiness," he assured.

"That will not be sufficient. I expect you to write every day. I want to know everything. I want to hear everything. I want to know what you are thinking … about everything. And you will stockpile all those letters, and when you come to shore, you shall have at least a dozen letters to send to me. Do not neglect quantity."

"My captain is not so strict."

"*I* will not have mutiny and floggings to keep *me* entertained, so time will pass much more slowly on my side, and you must attend to me on this matter, Lieutenant."

He tilted his head at this old formality.

"Frederick," I relented, gladly.

"You may depend on those letters. Farewell, dearest Jane."

I watched him drive away with the most curious mixture of elation and sorrow, and made my way back into the cottage in something of a daze. My father was examining the gift.

"It is a rather heavy thing. What do we think it is?" he wondered.

"Books, perhaps," Cassie speculated. "He was so very generous with his library."

I took the package. Good Heavens, it *was* heavy. I savoured the mystery and would have delayed it for hours, that I might have something to look forward to. But the family was waiting expectantly, so I began to unwrap it.

"Perhaps a few bottles of wine. It is a very tall box," Mama guessed.

I finally flipped the top lid over, and gasped at the bounty within. It was paper. Good quality paper ... some fifteen inches high. Enough for a year. Enough for two years. Stories, letters. A new novel, certainly, by this time next year. No other gift would have pleased me more.

"What is it?" Mama commanded.

I wordlessly brought out a thick pile of paper. I cared not whether the gift lived up to their expectations. But as I looked from one face to another, there were only smiles and nods of approval. They understood.

◇◇◇

Our own departure was soon upon us and passed in whirlwind fashion. Mr. Shaw was smothered with gratitude,

Martha was covered with kisses, and the sea and I bid one another adieu ... until Lyme.

It was but two days' journey to reach Bath. I could vaguely remember the distaste I had once felt at the prospect of moving there; so stuffy and demanding. But my days in Bath already felt numbered. Bath was not home, but holiday, and could thus be fully and thoroughly enjoyed. The city seemed intent on welcoming us, for there was a glorious parade, but three days after our arrival. We came across it quite by chance. What luck the entire family was about. We were greeted by the sight of jugglers, acrobats, clowns and musicians. I should blush at my own self-importance, but it felt like a spectacle put on for my benefit, as if the whole world wanted to celebrate my newfound happiness. I was an honoured guest and my hosts went to all lengths in their attempts to please me. And how well they succeeded. I clapped and tapped my toes, and laughed at the absurd displays. Cassie was quick to tease.

"Can this be the young woman who loathed the idea of being in Bath?"

"You will broil in hell for spreading such falsehoods," I scolded. "Bath is an incandescent place."

"But it is not Lyme," Cassie noted astutely.

Certainly not. I had yet to even set my eyes on Lyme. Nonetheless, it was already as dear to me as Steventon. For in that future home, all my hopes resided.

"Bath is but a waiting room, and a delightful one at that. For *your* sake, I hope it proves to be a most satisfying residence. For me, it is a temporary perch, and a hospitable one at that."

"I am unused to seeing you in such good spirits," Cassie marveled. She reached for my hand and gave it a tender squeeze. "It is long overdue," she sighed.

I could only agree. "But worth the wait," I added.

◇◇◇

Frederick's first letter arrived as punctually as I could have hoped for, in our second week in Bath. He had promised that he would send something before he boarded ship and I was now assured he would not neglect our correspondence. It was some two pages, a satisfying length. Some of the writing was a bit choppy and uneven, and I knew those sections had been written while he had been in a carriage.

> *Dearest Jane,*
>
> *I pray this letter finds you in the best of health, and that you and your family are now happily settled in Bath. Nothing of material interest has happened since our parting, so you must endure the outpourings of my heart. Perhaps you little realize the state I was in when we first met. I could no longer feel excitement or anticipation in contemplating my future. The Navy, my parish, the possibility of marriage ... all left me curiously indifferent. Even my mechanical designs, in which I took genuine satisfaction, did not provide real contentment.*
>
> *I had long ago abandoned faith in love. It seemed a childish dream that I was ashamed to have held onto for so long. I knew that I should likely marry, but the best*

I could look forward to was a companionable civility: a partner for the raising of offspring and the attendance of social engagements. Such a situation would be so relatively easy to find, I should not have to worry of disappointment.

So I resolved to settle for iron, and what should I stumble upon, but a chest full of gold. Do you know what a treasure you are?

It was very early in our acquaintance when I realized I was doomed to be bored by ladies I had previously found to be lovely perfection. So many of them resemble one another in admirable character qualities and beauty; I think I could search a lifetime and never find your like. You are a blue diamond atop a pile of granite. Or rarer still. A piece of fallen star, which cannot be matched with anything else upon the earth.

How astonishing! I did not want to devour the letter in one sitting. Especially since it could be a month or two before the next bundle of letters arrived. I forced my eyes back to the beginning, read it with growing enjoyment and broke off again at the same point, to save for later. Like a delicious confection, too good to consume all in one piece.

◇◇◇

A great deal of our time in Bath was necessarily spent with our relatives. James Leigh-Perrot was my mother's brother, and quite wealthy, owing to the combined inheritances of himself and his wife. But Mrs. Leigh-Perrot had brought more than fortune to the union. She brought ancestry of the highest order. The Austens had long been amused by the accounts of nobility by which we were distantly connected by way of Mrs. Leigh-Perrot. It had been a little bit thrilling, particularly when we were younger, to think that we should one day be wined and dined in royal circles. Perhaps have tea with the King himself. These fantasies had long evaporated, and I can only imagine the royal horror should a distantly related clergyman's family show up on the royal doorsteps. The connection had so little utility in our future prospects that it had taken on the role of an entertaining myth. But not so for Mrs. Leigh-Perrot. To her, it was the very foundation of her family's identity, and incontestably, her favorite topic of conversation.

But that was not what I wanted to hear discussed. I would much prefer to hear more of the deepest scandal that has ever shaken my extensive family and of which Mrs. Leigh-Perrot played the central role. For two years ago, she had been accused of shoplifting a piece of lace, and the lace, which had not been paid for, had been found in one of her parcels. She had been put in prison for eight months awaiting trial! I had never truly liked my aunt. Her arrogance and condescending nature had always worn on me. But we could not help but pity her. Cassie and I wanted to visit, but Mrs. Leigh-Perrot would not hear of two respectable young women visiting a prison.

While his wife was imprisoned, Mr. Leigh-Perrot had received a number of demands for money from the sales clerk in exchange for dropping the charges. As it turned out, this clerk had made a habit of slipping unpaid items into the pockets and bags of several customers, charging them with theft, and then trying to extort money. All of this became clear during the trial, where our aunt was finally acquitted.

I heard all of the details secondhand, and was most curious to hear her own account. But it was Mrs. Leigh-Perrot's estimation that it should never have happened. And therefore, it had not. She would never discuss it.

Thus, the conversation revolved around the family ancestry, the myriad accomplishments of the Austen male offspring, and the painful eruptions of my uncle's gout. Ah, well. My uncle had made me presents of so many wonderful books over the years that I could well endure his medical woes. But all in all, I was increasingly glad that my stay in Bath should be of relatively short duration.

The childless state of the Leigh-Perrots had always been the object of some curiosity. It is one thing for a married couple to find themselves alone in their middle years, after all offspring have been dispatched, but the Leigh-Perrot family had numbered two for over thirty years. The absence of noise and nonsense and games and mischief was sad to envision. But better no children than only one, for it would have been a lonely little thing, however well-versed in the family's noble lineage.

Back home after a long evening with the Leigh-Perrots, Cassie and I weighed the benefits and liabilities of this family connection.

"I always felt they were remiss in not providing us with any cousins," I began.

"It has hurt them more than it hurts us," Cassie reminded. "Truth be told, it has helped us, somewhat."

The absence of a Leigh-Perrot heir meant that the Austens were likely to figure prominently in the Leigh-

Perrots final bequests, a fact that had always provided Mama with great comfort.

"Besides, I thought perhaps you might envy their childless condition."

"No, indeed. A small number of children complete a family very nicely. It is only when procreation gets out of hand, that I have strenuous objections. Three or four children is a good size; six at most."

"Not thirty-two?" Cassie teased.

Good heavens. There had been an incredible story in the newspaper a few years back about a woman who had safely delivered her thirty-second child! And to the same husband. Cassie and I calculated that a marriage at the age of sixteen and one child a year until the age of forty eight would have to approximate her circumstances.

"If that woman had occasion to slip some arsenic into her husband's supper, I should personally hold her blameless. After all, we are not prize sows." I declared.

"I am sure she has no regrets," Cassie argued. "She must love the last as much as the first."

"Do not pretend you would have wished for such a thing. Even ten is distasteful, admit it."

"We shall see how you feel on the matter in ten years' time, Jane. In the meantime, there will be other matters to attend to, such as when, where, and who to invite …"

Ah, wedding plans. Quite premature, but still a lovely way to pass the time.

"I hope his entire family will attend," I mused.

"Will Mrs. Doherty receive an invitation?" Cassie inquired.

"Of course. She will not come, so there is no harm in inviting her. She cannot then spend till the end of her days complaining about the slight. She will continue, however, to curse the day that chance threw me in the path of her nephew."

"Chance you call it! It was not chance that directed us to Sidmouth."

J was astonished. "Take credit, do you?"

"Entirely."

"How could you have known? On that inauspicious day in the Godmersham parlour, with me abusing the lieutenant without mercy? How could you even have suspected?"

"I do not write stories, Jane. But that does not mean I lack imagination," she beamed triumphantly. "Moreover, I could not have *this* go to waste."

She went to her trunk in the corner of the room, and pulled out a beautiful white lacy dress folded neatly on top. Her wedding gown. She came to sit beside me and held the dress against me.

"You are an inch shorter, but it will not require much alteration."

"Cassie," I protested.

"I am glad I held onto it. It used to be very hard to look at it. But now the sight of it makes me very happy. It makes me think of the beach at Lyme. Where I hope to be a frequent visitor. A very frequent visitor." We held each other with one hand and held the dress between us with the other: a talisman to secure our future happiness.

CHAPTER THIRTEEN
A LETTER AT LAST

We had been in Bath for two months and the highly anticipated collection of letters had failed to arrive. The first several weeks, I had known better than to fixate on the daily mail delivery. After all, Frederick was thoroughly engaged in weighty matters of warfare. But they must touch land from time to time to refresh their supplies. Boxes of letters from the officers and entire crew would be sent out, without fail. For there were important military communications that had to be dispatched, and all personal correspondence would benefit from being bundled with them.

I had sent off four letters to him. I knew that it would be a more complicated matter for my missives to find *him*, for my address was stationary and his was afloat. But however long it should take to reach him, I was determined that he should have something to keep him company on those stormy nights. Something to console after harrowing battles and fallen comrades. I wanted to provide every reassurance of my feelings, and to let him know how deeply I had felt his own words to me. But two months had violated the natural limits of my patience. Until after the daily mail had been accounted for, my mind could fix on nothing else.

One of Bath's finer assets was the abundance of theatre performances and concerts to be had. Not so numerous as London, certainly, but enough to provide a constant stream of entertainment, and some diverting relief from my insufferable waiting.

I had loved the theatre for some ten or twelve years before I ever sat down in a real playhouse. For amateur neighborhood theatricals had been the rage in Steventon, and we had been invited on many occasions to join our numbers with Mrs. Lefroy's family, their parlour being much more spacious than ours. I had thus not only witnessed, but performed in such works as The Sultan, The School for Scandal, and High Life Below Stairs. I flatter myself to recall that my acting abilities were regarded as an invaluable asset to these productions. Indeed, we were so greatly entertained by creating our own amusements, I did not know if the experience of theatre as only a spectator should be as satisfying. Well, it was a different pleasure, but I looked forward to it greatly. We went to as many plays that winter as our budget would allow; Lover's Vows was one of my favorites of the season.

In addition, we were often at the loveliest concerts. I could never dream of recreating the works of Haydn or Mozart on my pianoforte, but I listened with rapt attention in the concert hall. Moreover, there were singers of some renown, most notably Madame Mara, whose voice helped transport one from all earthly cares.

I did my utmost to fixate on these diversions. But by mid-winter, my nagging impatience had become a daily anxiety. One snowy Sunday, coming home from church, Cassie and I walked somewhat ahead of our parents, the snow slowing all of us down.

"It is the first of February," I noted listlessly.

"The roads are terrible, Jane. And the post ... well, they do their best, but you know sometimes entire bags go astray. And the letters are not recovered for months. Or perhaps he is ill. Recall how we did not hear from Frank for almost four months when he had influenza. Such things happen frequently at sea."

Dear Cassie. I know she meant to comfort. But how desperate for a rational explanation was I, that I should be relieved to find out that Frederick was bedridden with fever or infection. What a thing to hope for.

"It need not be something serious," Cassie amended.

Was that to be my consoling hope, that he be ill enough to excuse his silence, but not ill enough to be in any danger? The perfect degree of indisposition.

"I wonder if he ever wrote to his parents about me. If he gave them a faithful account of my character, they might have cautioned him that he has acted in too much haste."

"I could not believe that for an instant," Cassie countered.

"Yet, he anticipated that his father and I might not be in accord," I recalled.

Who could tell where the truth lay? I grasped at straws. I spun fanciful scenarios. I fabricated. I distracted. And I despaired.

By the end of March, the hope had drained out of me and not an ounce remained. My bedtime sobs roused Cassie out of her sleep.

"Jane! Jane!"

She reached out to find me in the dark and threw her arms around my pitiable figure.

"I shall never see him again," I moaned, doubled over with the certainty of it.

"Do not lose hope. You cannot still fear that his family could talk him out of his love for you?"

"No. He does love me. I am sure of it. He would never abandon me."

"Indeed, no," Cassie assured.

"And so ... there is only one thing that would keep him from me."

"No! You must not think it. Do not even think it," Cassie pleaded.

She was frantic to spare me the loss that she herself had suffered. But it was beyond her power. Beyond prayer and hopes and all human efforts. He was gone. Of that, there could be no doubt.

◇◇◇

Two weeks later, shortly after tea, the mail arrived.

"You have a letter, Jane," Mama announced.

Cassie jumped and let out an audible sigh of relief. For one small moment, I allowed myself to hope. Then my mother placed the letter in my hands and I could see that it was from his brother, Dr. Barnes. I let the letter slide to the floor, and wordlessly headed for my bedroom. I did not need to read Dr. Barnes' letter. I knew what was within.

I perched on the edge of my bed. The thought of his lifeless body took me close to the brink of madness. For I think grief must be a branch of madness. It left me in convulsions and there seemed little escape. I wanted to run, as I had run as a child. Far and fast, and to such exhaustion, I could no longer stand. With no energy remaining for torturous and relentless thoughts.

It was another fifteen minutes before Cassie entered the room. Her tear-stained face was unnecessary confirmation.

"When did he die?"

Cassie spoke with forced calm, trying to steady us both. "October. Dr. Barnes wanted to write you as soon as he knew, but he did not have our address, and had to wait until the family was sent his journal and possessions."

"Buried at sea. And no grave to visit."

"Oh, Jane."

"I have been deceived before in a man's regard. But I did not imagine his love. I knew he would not leave me. I *knew* he would not leave me."

Cassie threw herself into my arms, full of heartbreak.

"I knew he would not leave me."

CHAPTER FOURTEEN
HAPPY ENDINGS

I exerted myself. I had to, for Cassie's sake. She was in such misery on my behalf. We clung tightly to one another. Neither of us had reached our wedding day, but we were widows all the same.

I had three dresses of mourning, which had been necessitated by the death of Cassie's fiancé. I had worn them the better part of six months, beyond the requirements of social convention, so that Cassie would know how much my heart was with her. Those black dresses had sat at the bottom of a trunk for years now, and though I had known they must be pulled out again one day, I could not have conceived of the abyss of grief that would accompany them.

I was at a great loss for something to do. There was no funeral. There was no memorial service. No visits from mutual friends and acquaintances. Cassie took over the chore of writing to Dr. Barnes to let him know that his letter had been received. I was in a listless, purposeless, languor. Mama would not hear of me skipping a meal, but every plate of food remained half full, every spoon to my lips required such effort. There was one thing however, I soon realized I should force myself to do ... so that I could put it away in a trunk, and never look on it again.

> *Elizabeth and Jane Bennet walked the streets of London. Jane Bennet entered a spice shop, and Elizabeth waited outside, glancing around indifferently. Then dumbstruck, she drew a sharp breath. Jane returned with a small package.*
>
> *"It is fortunate that we happened to be passing by today, for some of their stocks are quite low, and ..."*
>
> *Jane Bennet finally noticed that Elizabeth was staring across the street. When she turned in that direction, her stunned gaze soon matched her sister's. It was Darcy and Bingley, helping their wives out of a lovely carriage. Darcy gave a few quick orders to the driver, then arm-in-arm, the two couples strolled away. Jane Bennet exerted a determined smile.*
>
> *"I believe Aunt Gardiner said we shall have a roast tonight. I have been looking forward to it all day. We dare not keep them waiting."*
>
> *Dazed and resigned, Elizabeth allowed herself to be pulled away.*

There was nothing more to add, no artful conclusion. Just life's cold disappointments, resignation, and sorrow. And thus, I dispatched of the Bennet sisters. I piled all my manuscripts into a small trunk, and latched it with a padlock. I could not spare them another moment of thought.

My mind was continually filled, both with memories of the past, and promises for the future, that would never be kept. That Frederick and I would travel together: to London, Lyme, Cornwall, even abroad. That we should read together in the evenings, and enjoy exhilarating debates. That we would stand before one another undressed. And the embraces to follow. What shivers of anticipation I had felt at the prospect. Dreams that would remain dreams.

Mama assigned me the task of preparing the garden for the spring season. It was the smallest garden imaginable, and truly could be managed without any hired assistance. I was indifferent, but amenable. What else had I to do? I cleared away dead leaves and branches. And prepared a small herb patch, and rows of flowers. It gave me sufficient occupation and tired me enough to allow for some sleep at night. I was excused from all social engagements and my family seemed loathe to go out themselves and leave me without supervision. Whether I was reading or planting or eating, I could never look around without noting that I was under keen and sympathetic observation. And so the weeks passed.

At last I decided to accept Cassie's invitation for a long walk into the hills above the city. It would take the better part of the day, but the view was said to be incomparable. True enough. From that vantage point, Bath was a sight to behold, a stately and golden city. But worthy of no less admiration was my sister herself. I knew how attached she had been to Mr. Fowle, how happy, how expectant. And as deep and prolonged as her grief had been, I had also seen her recover herself. I had long wondered how she had done it. And now it was becoming clearer. The sensation of

Frederick's absence was being eased by a sense of his presence.

"I speak with him sometimes, in my head," I confided. "The conversations that we never had. That we would have had. Rather lively exchanges ... under the circumstances."

"Really, Jane! I spoke with Thomas too after he died. But I did not *argue* with him."

I shrugged, at last able to smile. "It was sport for us."

Cassie was glad to see I had arrived at memories that caused more pleasure than pain. We settled in the grass and assembled our little picnic lunch.

"You gave up all thought of marriage after Thomas died," I recalled. "And I was never able to see the sense in it, why you should not at least want to try and find love again."

"But now you know."

I did. "It has a sustaining power. To feel truly loved, but once ... it is enough." Thus, I was resolved to be at peace. With Cassie by my side, I had every chance.

We were not settled long when we began to hear the faint sounds of gunshots. Not hunters, surely, for the noise came from the direction of the city. And the shots grew in quantity. But what was the cause? Bath was no port city. There was little chance it was under attack. But wartime breeds dark fears, and we hurried back to uncover the truth. We saw people celebrating in the streets before we even heard the cause of it. "Cease-fire with France. Cease-fire with France." It was as a scene out of a dream that had taunted me for years. A dream that must have imposed itself on countless others as well. Reserved and fashionable Bath had lost all its restraint. There were hugs and weeping everywhere, and Cassie and I clung to one another in astonishment.

◇◇◇

The weeks following were filled with fireworks and dances and the flowing of wine from previously tightly rationed cellars. It was impossible to fully share in the joy around me, but I owed it to everyone, family and strangers alike, to celebrate for the sake of us all. I even agreed to attend a ball with my family; another invitation arranged by the Leigh-Perrots. I did not intend to dance and my mourning clothes protected me from all unwelcome advances. I was able to lounge in a low chaise by a warm fire and simply hear the music and allow the flames to mesmerize.

When I glanced away towards the swarming crowd, I saw glimpses of a familiar sight that made my heart stop. The crisply pressed trousers of a naval uniform. The officer's boots. The white gloves. The same build. The same stride. Had it all been some terrible mistake? Had he come back to me?

The figure emerged fully from the crowd, by my side, with gloved hand extended.

"May I have the honour of this dance? Or are you still opposed to the prospect of dancing with a brother?"

It was Frank. I threw myself into his arms, and had he not held me back so tightly, I would surely have sunken to the floor. For grief had weakened my body, and joy threatened to overwhelm it.

In short time, we were newly gladdened by the arrival of Charles. These two naval brothers who had caused their family such anxiety these past many years were finally safe and sound. From the moment Frank arrived, we could not bear to part with their company, and were up well past midnight, every night, demanding stories, be they riveting, mundane, or gruesome. We could be entertained by tales of peril, since we knew that all had been survived. We were in the highest of spirits. The youngest four children in the family back in the nest.

"Which one of you will oblige me to sit for a portrait tomorrow?" Cassie requested.

"Why not put all of us together in a single picture," I suggested. "For we are an uncommonly handsome family, are we not?"

My mother shook her head at such boasting, but how could she deny it? Our natural assets had been heightened by jubilation, and such family beauty should certainly be preserved for posterity.

At the end of every such boisterous and joyful evening, I would climb into bed with no expectation of rest. I waited until I could hear from Cassie's steady even breaths that she was soundly asleep. I would quietly steal to the fireplace, light a bedside candle, and pull out Frederick's letter. The only letter I ever had or ever would receive from him.

> *I am now at the Portsmouth harbor, savouring my last few hours of dry land. There is another fellow here awaiting the same transport. He has a violin and will doubtless know every sea shanty in all of maritime history. I asked him if he could manage a waltz. He laughed at me, for he knew that I was thinking of a lady, but was*

kind enough to oblige right there on the pier.

What memories it brought back of that night at the Assembly Hall. Not that music is required to bring back a multitude of vivid recollections. I summon them across every waking hour, and treasure every word, every picture, every thought, every communication. You will call me a man who is strangely entertained, but simply to recall your insults is enough to make me laugh. And it does not trouble me even to remember the painful misunderstandings, as they were so exquisitely resolved.

Many men who are on the verge of matrimony have called themselves the happiest of men. If ever I should hear this again, I shall pity the man and rally all charity to humour him. For I alone can claim that title. Farewell, dearest Jane.

From the happiest of men,
Your devoted Frederick

I cannot say that this nightly reading did not agitate. But it also never failed to comfort. How short our time together had been. But what a wealth of memories. You were not alone in your happiness, Frederick. And you will never be forgotten.

The letter was then gently put away. So very gently. For it must withstand the years.

◇◇◇

I had been meaning for some days to slip over to the chapel, for the most heartfelt expression of gratitude was in order. I chose a time when I knew the church should be sparsely populated. I timed my visit well, for I found myself quite alone, and could sit close to the altar, and say my prayers aloud.

"I grumble a great deal, and I lose sight of how good life has been to me. For do I not have the best of families? And Frank and Charles' safe return is a blessing for which we will never stop giving thanks. Although … after nine years of war, I think we were all hoping for something a bit more favorable."

But I had not come to complain. I meant to be a paragon of gratitude. "Still, to know a brief respite of life without war, it has made us all so very, very happy."

I laid my head down on the pew in front of me to rest. The excitement of recent late nights and a mind filled with tumultuous thoughts had blocked all efforts at sleep. Now the fatigue had caught up with me, and I drifted into a light fitful slumber: the kind where you speak to your *dreams*, but cannot break free of them.

Sobs erupted from the pew behind me; I instinctively knew the culprit without turning my head. It was Marianne Dashwood. How annoyingly self-indulgent she was. But I must own some responsibility as I have had full command of her improprieties. Why has she come to disturb me?

"There now. Can you not tell me what is the matter?" I briskly inquired.

"Willoughby is to marry another woman. I do not know how I shall go on without him," Marianne whined.

"Can you not see what a rake he was? I explained impatiently. "You are certainly better off without him. I thought I made that clear."

"He was the most charming and learned man of my acquaintance, with the deepest sensibilities," Marianne rhapsodized.

"If he had any true regard for you, he would not have run back off to Ireland ... ah ... that is to say ... he would have stayed and honoured your mutual devotion," I scolded.

My pronouncements were interrupted by a fresh eruption of weeping from another corner of the church. I was surprised to hear this commotion coming from Elinor Dashwood.

"This is unwarranted," I chided. "You are supposed to be the sensible one."

"Edward is to marry that dreadful Lucy Steele," Elinor cried.

"Well, would you prefer him to marry a lovely and virtuous woman?" I asked. I certainly would not. "There's less humour in it."

"Will you do nothing to relieve my torment?" she begged.

The thought of having to make any improvements was a taxing one, but perhaps, after all, could be quickly dispatched.

"All right. What if Lucy dies, and leaves Edward a widower, say, in five years' time?" I suggested.

My efforts went unappreciated and Elinor burst into a fresh storm of tears.

"What about me? Will you not reunite me with my love?" Marianne pleaded.

"With Willoughby? Never. And you ought to have more pride than to wish for such a thing."

My attention was drawn to more bawling from a few pews away. Elizabeth Bennet held a consoling arm around sister Jane Bennet. "Yes, yes, yes. Bingley and Darcy are married. It should hardly come as any great surprise," I declared.

"Why did love have to be snatched away so cruelly? Was it really so much to ask?" Elizabeth sighed.

"There are certain realities that must be faced by young women coming from such limited means." I explained, somewhat impatiently.

"To have married Bingley would have meant the deepest happiness imaginable," Jane Bennet pined.

"How often in this world is such happiness attained? I will not help to perpetuate these delusions," I avowed.

"And so you condemn us to solitude,

wretched loneliness, and unbearable regret?" Elizabeth Bennet anguished.

"Nonsense. You have each other ... your parents ... your ... health."

Jane Bennet broke into a fresh fit of tears. Elizabeth helped her gently to her feet. Enough. I marched to the back of the church, and turned around, quite unmoved.

Jane Bennet tried to soothe her sister. "Perhaps we angered her. What could we have done to deserve such a fate?"

How exasperating they were. How pitiable. "The world is full of spinsters. Why are you special?" I scolded.

Elizabeth's Bennet's eyes welled up with tears. "Were we never special to you?"

I was taken aback, and quite frankly, felt a stab of shame. Was there nothing in me but self-interest? Why should I condemn anyone else to unhappiness?

"Well ... nothing is set in stone," I conceded.

Elizabeth and Jane Bennet clasped hands, pleading, hopeful. I reached behind myself and opened the chapel door. In strolled Darcy and Bingley in formal attire. They joined Elizabeth and Jane Bennet at the altar, now both in wedding gowns. There was a full church to witness the double nuptials. A pastor stood before the two couples. Elizabeth turned to give me a quick backward glance of deep gratitude.

"We are gathered here to join this man and this woman, and this man and this woman in the bonds of holy matrimony. Which is not a state to enter into lightly or wantonly, but reverently, soberly, and in the fear of God."

The pastor's eyes fixed on mine, and in an instant, I found myself right in front of him. I turned to face my handsome bridegroom, Lieutenant Frederick Barnes, who looked as proud and happy as I could ever imagine him. Beside us stood Cassie and her Thomas Fowle, both glowing with anticipation. How fitting that Cassie and I should share this day of joy.

"You may kiss your brides."

Frederick drew close, bent down tenderly, and our lips finally met ... their long-awaited destiny. Such sweet warm devotion. I did not want it to end. Why should it ever have to end?

The heavy church door banged shut loudly and I was startled into wakefulness.

"Jane, you were not asleep, were you?" Cassie wondered.

"Certainly not. I was in prayer," I answered, sad to be torn away from my heavenly vision.

"I have good news," Cassie promised.

"And I have need of it."

"Martha will arrive on Friday," Cassie announced.

"Cassie! That *is* marvelous news. Oh, it has been almost

a full year since she has been with us."

I hastened down the church aisle and seized Cassie by the arm.

"How happy she will be to see Frank and Charles. We must go and ready her room. Oh, and get another theatre ticket for Saturday."

We exited the church in a flurry of excitement. How rich my life had become in all the truest blessings: family and friendship, and the warm memory of love. I would be forever grateful. And I would not mind at all to be visited again by such lovely dreams. But in the meanwhile, I should unlock that trunk of manuscripts. Perhaps there might be time to make a few improvements before Martha's arrival ...

POST SCRIPT

Jane Austen never married.

She revised *Sense and Sensibility* (presumably to her heroines' satisfaction) and published in 1811. *Pride and Prejudice* became a best-seller two years later.

Ten years after Jane Austen's death, 63 old Martha Lloyd married Jane's widowed brother, Admiral Frank Austen, avoiding both a lifetime of spinsterhood AND excessive reproductive burdens — a happy ending Jane would have loved.

AUTHOR'S NOTE

How much was Jane and how much was me? I drew on both Jane Austen's letters and her novels to get a sense of her personality, her values, and her voice. When Jane says, "I was as civil to him as his bad breath would allow," that line was taken straight out of one of her letters, although directed at a different person. But it's a good example of Jane's unapologetically blunt nature, which I tried to capture throughout. (There might be a half dozen lines pulled directly from her letters, and obviously, a multitude of references coming from her novels.)

The majority of the dialogue and all of the details surrounding Jane and Frederick are my best guess and best hope of what might have transpired.

◇◇◇

IT WOULD BE GREAT IF YOU'D LIKE TO LEAVE A REVIEW. GO TO MY WEBSITE FOR STORE LINKS.

◇◇◇

You can also sign up to be notified of new releases and sneak peeks. Or just drop me a line.

http://www.carolynvmurray.com

◇◇◇

Made in the USA
Middletown, DE
20 November 2017